Family Literacy:
Directions in Research and Implications for Practice

Summary and Papers of a National Symposium

**Edited by L. Ann Benjamin
and Jerome Lord**

**Sponsored by the U.S. Department of Education
Office of Educational Research and Improvement
in Collaboration with
the Office of Vocational and Adult Education
and the Office of Elementary and Secondary Education's Even Start Program**

For sale by the U.S. Government Printing Office
Superintendent of Documents, Mail Stop: SSOP, Washington, DC 20402-9328
ISBN 0-16-048460-X

U.S. Department of Education
Richard W. Riley
Secretary

Office of Educational Research and Improvement
Sharon P. Robinson
Assistant Secretary

National Institute on Early Childhood
      Development and Education

National Institute on Postsecondary Education, Libraries,
      and Lifelong Learning

National Even Start Program, Office of Elementary and
      Secondary Education

Office of Vocational and Adult Education

Conference Planners:

L. Ann Benjamin
Jerome Lord
Lenore Webb
Rita Kirshstein
Rebecca Shulman

Cover Artist: Katherine Van Horne

This report was prepared in part by Pelavin Research Institute under Contract Number RR 940290. The views expressed in this report represent those of the authors and do not necessarily reflect the opinions of the U.S. Department of Education.

January 1996

Foreword

Never before has education been more important to the well-being of the U.S. family, the fate of the country's economy, and the vitality of American democracy. No matter our age or socio-economic status, we all confront dramatic social, cultural, technological, and individual changes that demand more and better education for all. As a result of change and challenge, states are raising their academic standards; the workplace is fast becoming an increasingly sophisticated and technologically complex experience that requires the improvement of basic skills and the development of new skills. Daily life, then, demands, as never before, full literacy for all family members.

The U.S. Department of Education, under the leadership of Secretary Richard Riley, has supported and expanded reforms designed to broaden every family's access to education. From pre-school programs to adult education, and family literacy programs such as Even Start, we have worked with state and local governments, with the business community, and with health care organizations, to bring to all of our country's citizens a better quality of life through better education.

The Department's Office of Educational Research and Improvement (OERI) plays a critical role in this campaign. One of our jobs is to produce research and information on innovative programs and practices, including substantive, creative, "user-friendly" research that is especially important in the emerging field of family literacy. Our goal is to accelerate progress toward the day when the family is a miniature learning community in which there is shared devotion to helping one another to enhance family skills in reading, writing, numeracy, communication, and problem solving. Should families beset by difficulties and deprivations be unable to master these essential skills adequately, family literacy programs offer opportunity, support, and hope; and research aids in identifying the most effective means of helping family members to help one another by nourishing the potential of every family member—and fostering the conditions that promote both intellectual and emotional growth.

This publication represents an important step in developing a family literacy research agenda. It shows that the key consensus is the conviction that we must close the chasm between research and practice.

Sharon P. Robinson
Assistant Secretary
Office of Educational Research and Improvement

Acknowledgments

We would like to thank the many people whose support and encouragement helped us in planning the symposium and in preparing this report. We are especially grateful to the parents and staff of the Prince George's County, Maryland, Even Start projects who shared their lives with us and their perspectives on how family literacy programs can make a positive difference for families.

We gratefully acknowledge the financial assistance received from the Office of Elementary and Secondary Education's Even Start Program and the Office of Vocational and Adult Education and the commitment from Patricia McKee and Ronald Pugsley. We thank the authors and all who participated in the symposium; without their interest in family literacy and their knowledge and understanding of the issues, this project would not have been successful.

This was a collaborative project and, as with any strong collaboration, many people deserve our thanks for contributing to the work. We are especially grateful to Naomi Karp and David Boesel for their vision and constant support, to Maris Vinovskis for his great insight into research issues, to Veda Bright for her careful attention to details, to Bob LeGrand for his valuable editorial comments, to artist Katherine Van Horne for her sensitive family portrait that graces the cover of this report, and to the staff of Pelavin Research Institute for guiding the process and for helping us to meet our deadlines.

Table of Contents

Introduction

In early 1995, staff members at the U.S. Department of Education's Office of Educational Research and Improvement (OERI) began a dialogue with researchers and practitioners on the subject of family literacy. What began as an informal trading of papers, articles, and other information, soon grew into a project and a mission. The purpose of the project was to bring together as much existing information on the subject of literacy—especially family literacy—as possible. The mission—the first federal effort of its kind to be attempted on a nationwide scale—was to take the existing research and life experience available now and to synthesize that information into a "road map" for practitioners, researchers, and for the millions of Americans who need our help to become full participants in society.

Providing educational support to any family, particularly to families who lack educational and economic resources, is an awesome challenge. It combines the need to establish a basis of support services with particular skills and strategies for dealing with a family's learning needs.

It has become increasingly clear that any family's stability and productivity are linked not only to employment and employability, but also to the education levels of family members. Some early childhood programs like Head Start and Even Start were designed to "break a cycle" before it began. Current family literacy research and practices focus attention on the proposition that the cycle of deprivation and distress that so often accompanies lower levels of literacy skills could at the very least be mitigated by effective interventions.

Family literacy can be thought of in at least two ways:

- as the set of oral, graphic, and symbolic means by which family members exchange and retain information and meaning; and

- as the general level at which family members use their writing, reading, computing, communication, and problem-solving skills to accomplish the various tasks of their daily lives.

Wherever the emphasis is placed, the goals of research and practice must ultimately be to further our understanding on family learning and improve the reading, writing, numeracy, communication, and problem-solving skills of both children and adults within the family. We recognize that the construction of a research agenda, therefore, must start with the assumption that any idea or program is only fundamentally sound when it has been tested. As yet, there is not a sufficient research base for existing programs in family literacy.

The changing demographics of the American family have presented many questions for which there are no easy answers. These questions involve

- the ways families acquire literacy and sustain literacy;

- the necessity of choosing and pursuing finite goals;

- the best ways to organize programs around those goals; and

- the most effective strategies for helping families achieve higher levels of literacy.

As we studied the extant work on family literacy and family literacy programs, it became apparent that we needed to help build bridges between family literacy and the existing research on family support, early childhood, special education, and adult learning research and practice.

In deciding to hold a symposium, we determined to take the first step in structuring an ongoing research agenda focused on family literacy. We designed a *Research Design Symposium on Family Literacy* to bring together practitioners and researchers to discuss common themes and issues.

The symposium was designed around categories of questions that would help the participants focus their dialogue. The questions were designed to

- define and characterize the family and a family's literacy;

- conceptualize and structure family literacy programs;

- further define the target populations;

- distinguish a family support program from a family literacy program;

- identify needed and effective services to strengthen programs; and

- combine strategies and resources in effective collaborations to shape and move the dialogue thematically.

While there are excellent sources of research-based information on intervention programs in early childhood, the study of family literacy programs remains limited. This is not surprising, as such programs have been established as a separate area of study only in the past decade. With help from such organizations as the National Center for Family Literacy and the National Center on Adult Literacy, study and evaluation have, however, grown in size and immediacy. In fact, several family literacy program evaluations have provided initial insight into program effects and goals.

We chose distinguished practitioners to participate, and we commissioned 10 papers from leading research scholars that served as background reading for the symposium discussion. We selected the authors and their paper topics to present knowledgeable perspectives on diverse but relevant themes that would address the most pressing concerns of the various stakeholders in family literacy and related fields.

The papers are published here, along with a summary of the symposium. The authors and corresponding titles of their papers are listed below, with a short summary of each paper:

- **Judith Alamprese**, *Integrated Services, Cross-Agency Collaboration, and Family Literacy*. Two levels of coordination operate within family literacy programs: within the construction of the program itself, and federal or state coordination of funding. There is very little research on coordination, although a theoretical framework exists that could be tested.

- **Richard Durán**, *English Immigrant Language Learners: Cultural Accommodation and Family Literacy*. Programs must accommodate the clients' cultures; this is often a real issue with immigrant families for whom English is a second language. Literacy is not just language—it is also a cultural understanding of reality. Currently, there is a mismatch between the services offered to families and their real needs, although ethnography could be used to understand the challenges of these immigrant families. It is *essential* to understand the families who are the recipients of family literacy programs.

- **Vivian L. Gadsden**, *Designing and Conducting Family Literacy Programs That Account for Racial, Ethnic, Religious, and Other Cultural Differences*. Families have strengths, and realistic goals can be constructed based on reading, writing, and other basic skills. It is important to understand how cultures draw from various traditions, as well as how people define themselves within their culture. Something meaningful to the client must be presented within the context of family literacy.

- **Beth Harry**, *Family Literacy Programs: Creating a Fit with Families of Children with Disabilities*. Programs, when dealing with families having members with special needs, must be supportive and not interfere with the support systems that families have already constructed. Staff must both observe and participate in family life in order to identify problems and formulate solutions. To find what is most beneficial, we must consider the meaning of literacy, and how it can be used in tandem with families' already existing beliefs and practices.

- Andrew Hayes, *Longitudinal Study of Family Literacy Program Outcomes.* Longitudinal studies must be purposeful, and they must aim either to evaluate a program or to answer specific research questions. Researchers should focus on the problems, not the symptoms. They should consider the complexity of the audience, as well as whether they will focus on how people *may* make decisions, or how they *will* make decisions.

- Larry Mikulecky, *Family Literacy: Parent and Child Interactions.* Research shows which parental teaching strategies work better and which are less effective. *How* this information is used is critical. Family literacy can work, and does work, in some instances, with quality control. It does not work when resources are over-extended.

- Douglas Powell, *Teaching Parenting and Basic Skills to Parents: What We Know.* Programs designed to change parenting behavior indicate success in several different ways: allowing parents to integrate new ideas with pre-existing beliefs; acknowledging the relationship between parenting and other individual functioning; tailoring information and skills to the parents' reality, including their relationship with their children; keeping the focus on parenting; and providing long-term, intensive programs.

- Catherine Snow and Patton Tabors, *Intergenerational Transfer of Literacy.* What goes on in the family around literacy learning? Positive affect is important. Physical closeness and individual attention can contribute. Although a child's simple literacy skills may be sufficient for the first few grades of school, this does not always translate to the comprehension necessary by third grade. It is clear that different outcomes occur or manifest themselves at different stages, and that there are many levels for characterizing what happens between parents and children concerning literacy.

- Robert St. Pierre and Jean Layzer, *Informing Approaches to Serving Families in Family Literacy Programs: Lessons From Other Family Intervention Programs.* The research on family literacy programs shows that, while some small positive effects are in evidence among participating mothers and children, there are no large effects. The broader research on family interventions reveals that high-quality, high-intensity programs produce large effects. Family literacy should support programs aiming for large effects; although fewer clients will benefit, they will benefit more completely.

- Dorothy Strickland, *Meeting the Needs of Families in Family Literacy Programs.* Family needs must be identified and related to the program design. It is important to have a specific plan to address needs in an ongoing way. Also, programs should be client-driven, and clients should be involved in the evaluation process. Their needs mandate a flexible program structure.

This publication lays the foundation for researchers, practitioners, *and* policymakers to continue constructing a family literacy research agenda. The agenda-setting process is ongoing and must continue so that we can broaden the knowledge base and improve services and outcomes for families.

L. Ann Benjamin
National Institute on Early Childhood Development and Education

Jerome Lord
National Institute on Postsecondary Education, Libraries, and Lifelong Learning

Summary of the Research Design Symposium on Family Literacy

On September 7 and 8, 1995, researchers, practitioners, and policymakers gathered to assist the U.S. Department of Education in developing its research agenda in family literacy. The *Research Design Symposium on Family Literacy* was sponsored by the National Institute on Postsecondary Education, Libraries, and Lifelong Learning (PLLI) and the National Institute on Early Childhood Development and Education (ECI) of the Office of Educational Research and Improvement (OERI), and was held at Pelavin Research Institute's Conference Center in Washington, D.C. The Office of Elementary and Secondary Education's Even Start program, which sponsors family literacy projects that integrate early childhood education, parenting education, and adult basic education for disadvantaged families with young children, and the Office of Vocational and Adult Education, which funds the state-administered adult education program, provided support. The symposium was attended by experts in a variety of related areas, including adult education, early childhood education, learning disabilities and other disabilities, reading, sociology, English as a second language, family support, migrant education, program evaluation, and job training and workplace literacy.

Two themes stressed in opening remarks by the acting directors of PLLI and ECI set the tone for the meeting. Naomi Karp, Acting Director of ECI, called upon participants to begin a dialogue for producing a research agenda rooted in the assumption that all children and families have strengths. It is the responsibility of family literacy programs, she added, to help families identify and build on their strengths, and research should be conducted *with* and *for*, not *on*, families. Participants also were asked to identify the characteristics and qualities associated with successful programs, and to use this knowledge in generating successful family literacy programs. David Boesel, Acting Director of PLLI, noted that traditional adult basic education and General Educational Development (GED) programs have had difficulty attracting participation, while English as a second language classes are often

oversubscribed. What is the difference between these programs, he asked, and how can family literacy programs be modeled after programs that are considered successful? In addition, how can the effectiveness of family literacy programs be documented? These are important questions for both researchers and practitioners to address.

For practical as well as conceptual reasons, the symposium was structured around five informative sessions, accompanied by at least one question to stimulate debate, as follows:

- **Assumptions and Perceptions About Family Literacy**
  - *What basic assumptions and perceptions underlie our conceptions about families, literacy, and the clients served by family literacy programs?*

- **What We Know From Research and Practice and How We Know It**
  - *What do we know about research and practice in family literacy?*
  - *How do we know what we know about research and practice?*
  - *To what extent do research and practice reflect assumptions about family literacy?*

- **Defining the Characteristics of Family Literacy Programs**
  - *What makes family literacy programs unique from other kinds of programs that attempt to serve families in some way (e.g., in terms of strategies, program content, and structure)?*

- **Looking to the Future: Arguing for the Top Priorities for Research and Practice**
  - *What are the fundamental areas, issues, and questions surrounding family literacy as an area of inquiry as well as programmatic effort (e.g., evaluation issues, literacy at home vs. school, how clients perceive need)?*

- **Refining and Articulating Our Top Priorities for Research and Practice**
  - *What should be the top priorities for establishing a research and practice agenda?*

Assumptions and Perceptions About Family Literacy

What basic assumptions shape conceptions of family literacy? The assumptions and definitions researchers and practitioners adopt will influence the direction they will go in establishing priorities in research and practice. Symposium participants' assumptions focused on concerns regarding the problems faced by many families—problems such as financial dependency and inaccessibility of support services—and a belief in the strength of education and literacy to address many of those problems.

Among the assumptions stated during discussion were the following:

- The basic structure of family literacy programs should continue to be the structure presently used in programs established by agencies, organizations and institutions: a caregiver, a child, and an instructor who is engaged in improving family members' literacy skills and teaching the caregiver parenting skills in a center and at home.

- All programs have some effects on participants that are intended and some effects that are not intended.

- Both intended and unintended effects are relatively equally distributed among participants and include some effects that last a short while and some that endure.

> *Although influenced by socio-cultural factors, communities, and the extended family, the family itself is, and should be, treated as the basic unit for literacy and learning.*

- Family literacy programs as presently structured and operating can be modeled, adapted, and disseminated in other sites and contexts.

- Providing coordinated, multi-faceted services to participants is more beneficial and effective than providing any single service.

- Most target families want to acquire higher levels of literacy for one or more members of their families.

- Parent/caregiver involvement with a child in learning activities is basically a very good thing for the child.

Defining Family Literacy

The definition of family literacy used by Even Start and Head Start includes the following components:

- interactive literacy activities between parents and their children;

- training for parents on how to be their children's primary teacher and to be full partners in the education of their children;

- parent literacy training; and

- early childhood education.

This definition translates into the provision of three core services to all families: parenting education, adult basic education, and early childhood education, with some activities provided with parents and children together and some instructional components taking place in the home.

Within the papers, researchers addressed in a variety of ways the need to define family literacy. Andrew Hayes, of the University of North Carolina-Wilmington, approached it by enumerating characteristics of "literate families." He noted for example, that literate families have the ability or means to

- acquire needed or desired information from printed verbal, symbolic, and graphic materials and from oral communications;

- communicate their intent or ideas to others in printed (written) verbal, oral verbal, graphic or symbolic forms;

- set short-term and long-term goals for self and family;

- implement plans for accomplishment of personal or family goals;

- make valid predictions of the probable effects of their actions or of family conditions on themselves and others; and

- support the development of family members, and help others in the family with their learning and development.

Richard Durán, of the University of California at Santa Barbara, noted that more than one way exists to interpret literacy. It is therefore important to put literacy in its particular context based on an understanding of how language, culture, and society are interconnected.

As it is most narrowly defined, literacy consists of basic reading skills. The broadest definition was put forth by several participants, who argued that literacy is a cultural concept—not merely a set of skills, but a way of thinking and behaving and responding to one's environment. Some definitions included computer literacy—a key skill in the marketplace, and therefore arguably an essential aspect of any

literacy program. Sharon Darling, of the National Center for Family Literacy, mentioned that family literacy is a term derived from a program that began as *intergenerational learning*. Many of the participants agreed that the concept of "family" should be defined broadly, as well, so as to include any intergenerational unit that includes at least one caregiver. As symposium moderator Dorothy Strickland, of Rutgers University, observed, "Things that seem ordinary are often difficult to define."

Characterizing Program Participants

Participants in family literacy programs are generally from at-risk families with little formal education. For example, to be eligible for Even Start, a family must have a low income and consist of at least one adult who is eligible for adult basic education and at least one child under the age of eight. Currently, many longstanding survival systems—such as dependence on the extended family and the community—are breaking down. Charles Geboe, with the Bureau of Indian Affairs, stressed the current severity of this problem among the American Indian population, leaving parents without a workable model for how to raise their children. Simultaneously, government support is quickly eroding. With these factors working against people, one question is, *How can family literacy programs offer a promising strategy to ameliorate problems of families?*

Everyone agreed families are not all alike, but all have individual identities and worth and have accumulated a great deal of history, or what Vivian Gadsden, of the National Center on Fathers and Families, terms "life text." All families, added Joyce Muhlestein, member of OERI's National Educational Research Policy and Priorities Board, have a learning family culture,

> *Significant changes in literacy, parenting behavior, and family dynamics appear when there is a commitment to long-term, intensive work with parents . . . . (B)oth duration and number of contacts are important in yielding more pervasive, sustained effects . . . . However, evidence suggests that parenting education or improvements in parents' circumstances, by themselves, will not result in improved child outcomes.*

although this culture may not be academic or literate in the traditional sense of the word. Although influenced by socio-cultural factors, communities, and the extended family, the family itself is, and should be, treated as the basic unit for literacy and learning. Literacy is tied to parenting behaviors—how family members see, use, and treat written, oral, and symbolic material; therefore, family literacy programs cannot work with children to the exclusion of parents. However, most practitioners agreed that family literacy programs are being driven by the educational needs of the adults within the family unit.

Beth Harry, of the University of Miami, emphasized that programs serving families with special needs should have the greatest respect for adaptive coping strategies that these families are already using. Vivian Gadsden reiterated that programs must encourage participants to see their family and social history as critical to their literacy development and the learning process.

Among the research findings or implications noted in the papers were that significant changes in literacy, parenting behavior, and family dynamics appear when there is a commitment to long-term, intensive work with parents; and that both duration and number of contacts are important in yielding more pervasive, sustained effects (see Powell; St. Pierre & Layzer; Hayes). It appears that guided opportunities for discussion among low-income parents facilitate change in their parenting attitudes and behavior (Powell; St. Pierre & Layzer; Gadsden). However, evidence suggests that parenting education or improvements in parents' circumstances, by themselves, will not result in improved child outcomes (Powell; St. Pierre & Layzer). This supports conclusions that efforts to improve outcomes for adults and children must be directly targeted to both groups, individually and collectively. Despite these concerns, it is widely believed that well-designed and well-executed family literacy programs can effect a positive change in families.

Concerns About Assumptions

Agreement on key assumptions proved problematic for symposium participants, in part because of the diversity of experiences and perspectives represented, and also because of concerns that their assumptions and ideas about what family literacy *should* be, might be confused with the kinds of assumptions upon which many unsuccessful family literacy programs base their practices.

Participants also mentioned some common assumptions about family literacy and related concepts that demand careful examination. Beth Harry stressed that although literacy is believed to be an essential tool for maneuvering in our society, many people with low-level literacy skills function very well without being literate. A basic assumption of family literacy programs is that they are successful as long as they do some good. Rhea Lawson, of the University of Wisconsin, challenged this assumption, asserting that barriers to success are built into many programs. These barriers include understaffing, lack of effective planning and evaluation, inadequate staff development, lack of cultural awareness and understanding, a focus on obtaining funds, and a lack of investment in the adults in the program. These problems may explain why programs can result in failure. Judy Alamprese, of COSMOS Corporation, observed that educators, as well as the general public, have tended to value the education of children above the education of adults. Instead, family literacy programs must value equally the education of both children and adults, and express this in terms of resources.

What We Know From Research and Practice and How We Know It

As we seek to apply research to practice, we must proceed with caution. Participants proposed that a great deal is known about family literacy and family literacy programs that has not yet been applied to such programs. However, as Larry Mikulecky, of Indiana University, cautioned, what has been shown to work for one program does not necessarily work for a large number of programs that may be poorly funded. Most funded programs are not based on research, and researchers often observe programs that are unsuccessful in achieving sizable gains in test scores for participants or in advancing their skill levels. Research to date shows that the development of literacy skills should be more closely tied to fundamental life skills, including those required for gainful employment. Research also should suggest strategies for moving people from welfare to work. A further complication is that practitioners often see the effects on families and on individual program participants that are never measured by researchers either during participation in programs or at any time thereafter.

Sources of Information

Symposium participants suggested a variety of sources of information to be tapped. For example, Andrew Hayes assured participants that a knowledge base in instructional design exists that can inform the development of program standards. This knowledge base can document who family literacy clients are (e.g., participants in Even Start programs and National Center for Family Literacy (NCFL) programs), how best to work with diverse groups, and the different levels of need encountered and accomplishment reached. Research through NCFL and on Even Start family literacy programs is beginning to be used to determine what program features result in the highest success rates. A great deal of research also can be borrowed from other fields—for example, the learning disabilities field has accrued at least seven different methods for teaching reading. This kind of information, too, needs to be circulated and put to use within the family literacy field.

The families themselves are an important source of information and can best speak to what they need and what works for them. "The participants are the real experts," said Mercedes Pérez de Colón, of Avance-Hasbro Family Resource Center in San Antonio. "Research will never tell you what participants can," she added. However, Andrew Hayes emphasized the difficulty in using families themselves to define programs. Ann

Kornblet, of the Learning Disabilities Association of America, countered that family literacy program staffs are not the best judge of what families need. Hayes and Kornblet agreed that there is a difference between symptoms and needs, and that it is the practitioner's duty to ensure that families receive the services and education they really need, not just those they think they need. By offering exposure, knowledge, and information to families, programs can prepare families to make decisions for themselves. Ultimately, family literacy staff need to work together with families to design a program that will build on participants' strengths.

From a practitioner's viewpoint, Howard Miller, Director of the Prince George's County, Maryland, Even Start program, also concluded that most of what we know about the delivery of family literacy programs is based on our own experiences in working with families. Programs are accountable for achieving observable goals; however, many programs do not have access to research literature in a usable form. Without this information, programs lack up-to-date information on what works, particularly in ways that enable them to demonstrate *long-term effects.*

Program Models

Programs often are modeled after existing programs that are considered to be successful, but they may not be based upon research findings and have not necessarily been able to document measurable improvements in family outcomes. For example, four elements of traditional family literacy programs are widely considered key, but their effects have not yet been fully measured over time:

- instruction for parents;

- instruction for children;

- support for parents and consideration of parenting issues; and

> *There was consensus . . . that one feature modeled by Even Start—the emphasis on building a relationship of trust between families and program staff—is absolutely essential.*

- time for parents and children to interact together.

Some participants argued that the lack of documented success was due to a failed understanding of how to successfully implement this design; others, such as Larry Mikulecky, argued that a deeper problem is that of idealistic program designs confounded by the reality of limited resources. For example, Even Start has been cast as a model program, even as it struggles to discover what its own best practices are. But there was consensus at the symposium that one feature modeled by Even Start—the emphasis on building a relationship of trust between families and program staff—is absolutely essential.

Family literacy as a concept is still considered to be in its infancy, particularly when compared to early childhood education, and even when compared to the adult basic education program. Gail Houle of the Office of Special Education Programs, asked, "Is family literacy at the point of identifying best practices?" The question has not yet been answered.

Defining the Characteristics of Family Literacy Programs

An important goal of the symposium was to identify the characteristics and qualities that distinguish family literacy programs from other programs serving families and to identify what makes family literacy programs successful. As financial resources tighten, the successful program characteristics determined by the participants become more important as a policymaking tool: programs may be judged and funded (or not funded) according to these characteristics. Currently, Judy Alamprese pointed out, funders do not have access to useful guidelines; characteristics of successful or effective family literacy programs can and should be presented to funders in a useful format. In addition, researchers suggested that it would be more effective to fund a few high-quality programs than to fund a greater number of programs with low budgets and minimal goals.

Clearly, literacy development is a key characteristic of any family literacy program. But, as Patton Tabors, of Harvard University, asked, is the goal of a family literacy program really to increase literacy? If it is, must it be for parents *and* children? Often self-esteem is raised, but not literacy. Adult education programs often must contend with these issues, as do many existing family literacy programs. Also, participants strongly urged that family literacy programs must deal with the questions of what to emphasize in the instructional component of the program (e.g., whether it is more important to teach job skills to parents, or to have them read to their children). Douglas Powell, of Purdue University, argued that programs should maintain a balanced, concrete focus on parenting and child development. Ultimately, while purposefully leaving literacy undefined, participants agreed that it is essential for a family literacy program to improve the literacy skills of both parents and children.

The central point is that, whatever else they might do, family literacy programs must serve as an extension of the family itself, rather than an extension of a school environment. Each program must involve collaboration, with both strong participant involvement and coordination of support services and funding sources across agencies. Several participants noted that widely recognized assumptions do not necessarily play out in practice. For example, although participants generally agreed that effective family literacy programs are characterized by a participant-driven approach—one in which participants are involved in the decision-making process and their stated needs drive program delivery and instruction—Dorothy Strickland maintained that programs often are not designed that way. Jean Layzer, of Abt Associates, countered that there is no research evidence that participant-driven programs are more effective than other kinds of programs. Rhea Lawson disagreed, stating there is evidence that if

> *Family literacy programs must serve as an extension of the family itself, rather than an extension of a school environment.*

participants are involved in planning, retention rates are higher. Howard Miller concluded, "We define literacy; let parents define the goals."

Defining Characteristics

Symposium participants proposed characteristics critical to family literacy programs. Programs must

- offer literacy development for parents and children;

- serve as an extension of the family, recognizing their individual differences;

- include strong participant involvement;

- coordinate support services and other sources of funding;

- establish a designated time and a process for a parent support system;

- include parent-child interaction;

- integrate learning and participation on three levels: parents, children, and parent-child;

- integrate core instructional components, total program services, and staff development;

- offer ongoing monitoring of quality by all stakeholders;

- define family broadly—intergenerational, including children and caregiver(s);

- offer program goals that consider other support systems and agencies and offer links to other services; and

> *A program that strives to teach and help families must also attend to the factors that might make it difficult for them to attend classes . . . . These services help support the families' educational needs, and can provide a bridge to success after the program's completion.*

- address long-term student goals.

Fran Tracy-Mumford, State Director of Adult Education for Delaware, along with Judy Alamprese, stressed the importance of integration and coordination in the delivery of family literacy programs. Core components, total program services, and staff development all must contribute to integration, not fragmentation. The inclusion of parent-child interaction, a parent support system, and the integration and coordination of parent curriculum, child curriculum, and parent-child curriculum, are also important. Robert Marley, of OERI's National Educational Research Policy and Priorities Board, added that staff development is crucial, as teachers and support staff are the backbone of a successful program. In addition, the program must be monitored by all stakeholders, including staff, outside entities, and clients.

Program Goals

The long-term goals of the clients also must be addressed. Although the idea of including technology (both computers and assistive technology) as a necessary aspect of the program was discussed, it was not included in the final list of defining characteristics generated by participants. However, most participants considered technology a very important aspect of family literacy—both as a tool of inclusion, and as a form of literacy in a modern, technological society. Gus Estrella, of the United Cerebral Palsy Associations, noted the tremendous benefits of assistive technology to individuals with disabilities. Without such assistance he would not have been able to participate in the symposium.

The subject of support systems fueled debate on what the focus of family literacy programs should be. Although participants agreed that program goals should consider other support systems and agencies and should provide links to them, many were wary of programs stretching themselves too thin. Families who are economically disadvantaged, especially those who would benefit from a literacy program, have many more problems and barriers to deal with besides improving their literacy skills. The need to survive often precludes the possibility of the family being organized to pursue educational goals. Therefore, a program that strives to teach and help families must also attend to the factors that might make it difficult for them to attend classes (e.g., transportation difficulties, health needs, lack of affordable child care). As the national evaluation of the Even Start Program and other research is beginning to show, these services help support the families' educational needs, and can provide a bridge to success after the program's completion. However, limited resources dictate that family literacy programs cannot do everything. As Jean Layzer stressed both in her paper and during the conference, research shows that only high-quality, high-intensity programs effect real change. Anything less leads to small effects or none at all — a result that shows a waste of money, and reflects poorly on family literacy programs.

Given these limitations, some participants argued, programs must focus on a particular goal—teaching literacy skills. It is likely that these skills, if successfully taught, will enable families to access other resources on their own. The conclusion, voiced by Lori Connors-Tadros, of Johns Hopkins University, was that we must accept both the narrow and broad definitions of family literacy.

Looking to the Future: Arguing for the Top Priorities for Research and Practice

Nearly every aspect of family literacy program design and effectiveness contains numerous unanswered questions. The participants listed a number of questions to orient future research. These questions tended to echo group concerns as well as prior discussion.

For the most part, they fell into one of six categories:

- family functioning;

- collaboration with support services;

- staff development practices;

- comprehensiveness and effectiveness of programs;

- effective program design strategies; and

- measurement of program effectiveness.

One of the challenges of the symposium participants was to confront the complexity of how families function. Assuming that something happens with a family's daily functioning that is fundamental to the initiation and the development of the literacy of its members, the participants raised the following questions:

- What is it about the relationship between parents and children around literacy activities at home that is crucial to program content in family literacy programs?

- How do parents and children learn, both together and separately, and does their interaction improve learning?

- What different methods do parents use in the exchange of literacy with their children?

- How does education in parenting skills affect the literacy skills of adults and children?

This last question sparked some concern about the underlying attempt to alter parenting behaviors according to a literacy model; at what point, one participant asked, does this become "cultural imperialism?"

Another area of concern was the *extent to which support services are an essential part of family*

> *Research shows that only high-quality, high-intensity programs effect real change. Anything less leads to small effects or none at all.*

literacy programs. Having already determined that availability of support services was a key characteristic of family literacy programs, the participants focused on questions of extent and structure:

- What is the difference in effectiveness between a stand-alone family literacy program and one that operates in conjunction with a number of other service agencies?

- How can the goals and structures of family literacy programs be included within already existing service institutions?

- What strategies are most effective for developing and sustaining interagency coordination?

- Ultimately, to what extent must a family literacy program be a family support program in order to be effective?

Staff development also is a key characteristic of family literacy programs.

- What can be used as a model for effective staff behavior?

- What staff development practices are most effective in preparing adult literacy instructors to be effective in family literacy?

Everyone involved with family literacy wants it to be as comprehensive as possible, but who is the target audience for these programs? Some participants were concerned about the literacy needs of adults and children with learning disorders and disabilities, and others worried about groups such as migrant workers and their families, and children and adults with physical disabilities.

- How do we target literacy skills to all client needs regardless of economic or cultural differences?

- How can we more efficiently design computer networks and assistive

technology to improve family literacy effectiveness and training?

A fifth set of questions focused on basic program design:

- How can we design interventions that capitalize on the existing beliefs and strengths of families?

- What roles should the clients themselves play in planning, implementing, and evaluating programs?

Finally, the topic of measuring effectiveness elicited several questions:

- How can we anticipate both positive and negative unintended consequences of programs, and how do we measure them?

- How do we measure best practices in family literacy?

- Ultimately, how do we know if family literacy programs work?

Research must focus not only on the *causes* of problems and their relationship to proposed interventions, but also on families' *natural literacy practices*, and on what those practices mean to the families, themselves, and how such practices change over time.

Refining and Articulating Our Top Priorities for Research and Practice

The *Research Design Symposium on Family Literacy* was a first step forward in that it brought together researchers, policymakers, and practitioners in one place at one time. One conclusion reached by participants was that research must be made accessible to practitioners; in this way, the collaboration between researchers and practitioners can be ongoing, and can then be shared with policymakers. Only this involved cooperation of all concerned parties will bridge the chasm of which Assistant Secretary Sharon Robinson spoke.

Through the questions and answers that were tendered, several key points came out:

- **Family literacy is perceived and defined differently** by practitioners, researchers, and families. Some consensus on what family literacy is must be reached. How it is defined will determine how programs approach evaluation, instruction, staff development, and program delivery.

- **All stakeholders** must strive to bring together the diverse perspectives and experiences represented in family literacy and related fields so that a common set of assumptions can be established that will inform the development of key research questions.

- **Researchers and practitioners** must determine how best to influence policy decisions.

- **Research must both substantiate** and inform practice. "I knew (what makes effective practice) before researchers knew it," said Delia Garcia, of Florida International University. Howard Miller emphasized, "We need new information" from researchers to improve practice. A major challenge is to develop a mechanism for getting research information back to family literacy programs.

- **Having state-of-the-art knowledge** does not guarantee that programs will use it. For example, even though researchers and practitioners may agree that use of technology in instruction, emphasis on a practitioner-driven approach, and a well-trained staff are important to the success of a program, many programs do not put their beliefs into practice. Limited resources, resistance to change, and misconceptions about how these tenets can be translated into practice may inhibit their adoption by individual programs.

- **Researchers and practitioners must devise** a way to determine when and to what extent change has taken place in achieving both short-term and long-term outcomes. That entails being clear about the end one wants to achieve.

- **We need to know more from states and localities about the impact** of their involvement in and interpretation of family literacy, as well as the impact of these and other factors on program design and funding.

In addition, the following questions are crucial in beginning to understand family participation in family literacy programs:

- How can researchers and practitioners design and implement programs that are more respectful of family and cultural differences, and that foster a sense of hope?

- What does it look like for family literacy providers to serve families *well*? Program administrators must be honest about what is feasible given limited resources. In the spirit of service and compassion for families in need, family literacy programs would like to serve everyone, but is that really serving families well? Program staff must choose how *comprehensively* families can be served with limited resources. Programs serving families also must address any mismatch between their perceptions about education and literacy and those of families, or between their institutional capital and family resources.

- What is the best way to influence changes in practice? Will programs be more easily influenced by the quality of information available from research and evaluation, or through advocacy? Might the answer to these questions be dependent, as Andrew Hayes suggests, on the notion that programs often base their decisions more on emotion than on objective information?

Next Steps

Researchers and practitioners may address all of the above issues in a variety of ways, including:

- convening in smaller groups focused on specific content or process areas;

- funding future research activities; and

- holding additional meetings or focus groups, and bringing individuals together at national conferences.

Also, Fran Tracy-Mumford highlighted the absence at this symposium of papers by practitioners, which would provide a different perspective from that of researchers. Similarly, Naomi Karp observed that participants in family literacy programs were not represented at the symposium and should be present in future discussions. What both indicate is that the development of a research agenda is not a static activity and must take into account changing concerns in any given field.

Integrated Services, Cross-Agency Collaboration, and Family Literacy

Judith Alamprese
COSMOS Corporation

Recent descriptive studies of family literacy programs highlight the importance of cross-agency collaboration. Collaboration among education and human service agencies in local communities has, in fact, emerged as a critical element of family literacy—in part because of the realization that the process of addressing the literacy needs of parents and children is complex and requires the delivery of multi-faceted services to meet those needs. In addition, family literacy intervention staff increasingly have identified the provision of integrated services as a necessary program component, and have used the collaborative process to build relationships among agencies delivering services.

The trend toward a reduction in education and social services funding also has prompted programs to work together in exchanging services and materials as a strategy for supporting comprehensive interventions. Family literacy programs have thus been creative in identifying the various resources in a community that may be used to develop an integrated approach, including education as well as family support services. Furthermore, cross-agency collaboration has been encouraged by the federal programs that authorize the expenditure of funds for family literacy, such as Even Start and Head Start. Finally, inherent in the delivery of any successful multi-component program is the coordination of agency staff representing the different service components.

While policymakers and practitioners consider cross-agency collaboration to be an essential ingredient of an effective family literacy program, there is little evidence concerning the relationship of collaborative activities to the functioning of these programs and the attainment of client outcomes. As an initial step in defining the research issues that should be addressed concerning the role and the impact of cross-agency collaboration and integrated services in family literacy programs, this paper presents a preliminary framework for examining the factors necessary to sustain collaborations in family literacy. The framework is drawn from the classical research on interorganizational relationships and from studies of interagency coordination in adult education and human services. Also discussed in the paper are the areas of inquiry that appear to be important for any understanding of the collaborative process and its outcomes for family literacy.

What Is Known About Collaboration in Family Literacy

Typology of Programs

Family and intergenerational literacy programs are being implemented in communities with varying durations and intensity of services. The four-component model developed as part of Kentucky's Parent and Child Education (PACE) program, and currently disseminated by the National Center for Family Literacy (NCFL) (1995), is a comprehensive approach to breaking the cycle of poverty and undereducation in the family system that calls for the integration of adult education,

> *Collaboration among education and human service agencies in local communities has . . . emerged as a critical element of family literacy in part because of the realization that the process of addressing the literacy needs of parents and children is complex and requires the delivery of multi-faceted services to meet those needs.*

early childhood education, parent and child interaction time, and parenting education and support. In the NCFL model, the four components are expected to work together in a flexible framework that meets the needs of parents and children.

Other intergenerational and family education models are being used that do not require the four components, but still are encouraging parents' and children's literacy development, directly or indirectly. One such model provides services to parents and their children with less intensity and duration than the NCFL model and with less focus on formal instruction. Other variations include the provision of literacy services to children indirectly, basically by enhancing parents' abilities to select books and to read to their children—or to serve children directly in supplemental reading programs wherein the role of the parent is to support children's literacy efforts, rather than to participate in adult literacy education (Nickse, 1991).

Local-Level Collaborations

Since few systematic studies of family literacy have addressed cross-agency collaboration (e.g., Quezada & Nickse, 1993; St. Pierre et al., 1993), most information about collaboration in family literacy must be drawn from handbooks and program reports (e.g., the Barbara Bush Foundation for Family Literacy, 1989; National Center for Family Literacy, 1991; Association for Community Based Education, 1993). While the majority of those documents do not describe the collaborative processes that are used by programs and the effects of those processes, they do provide information about the types of organizations involved in collaboration and the challenges faced in carrying out collaboration, and thus are an important data source for understanding the major players involved in collaboration.

Cross-agency collaboration has evolved at both the local and the state level. At the local level, education and human service agencies may work together to fund and to implement a family literacy program that reflects one of the service delivery models previously described. Even Start

and Head Start programs are working with local adult education service providers, for instance, in organizing family literacy programs that provide coordinated adult and early childhood education services. Within a program, staff from different service components collaborate in carrying out services that represent different levels of integration.

Cross-agency collaboration and the provision of integrated services are reported in all types of local programs, but are more likely to occur in the comprehensive approaches to family literacy. Integrated services can be considered to be one outcome of cross-agency collaboration, wherein two or more entities work together toward a common goal. In family literacy programs, integration can be defined in terms of the co-location of the delivery of services, the substantive integration of the adult and early childhood education curricula, the collaboration among staff from the different substantive components that comprise a program, the coordination of support services that are provided to parents through the program, and the coordination of funding sources to support a program. For example, in family literacy programs using the four-component model, it is optimal to have co-located adult education and early childhood education services to facilitate the parent-child interaction time.

Such services as the above may be directed by the same agency, as was found in about half of the Even Start programs examined in the national evaluation, or they may be provided in cooperation with other agencies or through contractual relationships with other agencies (St. Pierre et al., 1993).

Another form of integration involves the curricula used for both parents and children. In programs where curricula integration is a goal, instructors from the adult and early childhood education components meet to plan curriculum and to schedule activities that reinforce desired concepts in both instructional programs. The Family Literacy Demonstration Project, a collaborative effort between the Center for Literacy and the Philadelphia Public Schools, is an example of instructional content for adults mirroring the K-12 curriculum for children. As children were learning classification using shapes and colors, adults worked on the classification of different types of literature (National Institute for Literacy, 1993).

The importance of providing integrated support services to families in order to assist them in dealing with barriers to participation is a common theme in descriptions of family literacy efforts. While noting the critical role of these services in more general family support programs, researchers have acknowledged the difficulty of evaluating the impact of such services on family functioning (e.g., Kagan & Shelley, 1987; Weiss, 1988). In family literacy programs, the emerging pattern is one wherein programs either provide support services directly to clients or work in conjunction with existing networks, such as child care, employment training, and other family support services (Brizius & Foster, 1993). The 10 projects cited in the Barbara Bush Foundation for Family Literacy handbook (1989) illustrate the range of support services that are being offered as part of family literacy programs, including the commonly provided services of transportation and meals as well as lending libraries and stipends for purchasing reading materials, pre-employment training, and medical and dental exams.

The coordination of funding sources is one of the more difficult aspects of operating family literacy programs. Often the adult education program and the Even Start or Head Start agencies in a given community have no prior working relationship, and their ability to offer joint programming is problematic. In an effort to promote coordinated funding, the NCFL has structured its demonstration programs to require matched funding, which encourages the family literacy program to seek support from community agencies that, indeed, can contribute to the program's services.

The issue of coordinated funding for education and human services has been discussed extensively at the federal level, and recent research indicates that local coordination of funding is facilitated when the state offices administering those funds provide technical assistance and encouragement to local agencies (Alamprese, Brigham & Sivilli, 1992). As block grants become more important,

the issue of the types of services that are authorized under federal or state programs will be more critical. Resources such as those provided by the NCFL in describing the possible funding sources for family literacy have assisted local programs in organizing their solicitation strategy. As the types of funding and procedures for accessing money change, further assistance will be needed to provide local programs with access to multiple funding sources.

In carrying out a variety of integrated services, family literacy programs have had to develop collaborative relationships with other agencies and organizations in a community that may include the immediate exchange of goods or a longer-term commitment to working together in coordinating services and funding. While the conventional wisdom of family literacy providers is that collaboration is an essential element of any program, it is widely recognized that effective collaborations are difficult to implement and sustain. The analysis of early data from the Even Start evaluation noted that while 123 projects were involved in 2,128 cooperative arrangements to provide core program services, there were a number of barriers to implementation including problems of communication and coordination and difficulties in structuring support services (St. Pierre et al., 1993). These barriers are echoed in other studies of family literacy and intergenerational programs (e.g., Association for Community Based Education, 1993; Quezada & Nickse, 1993).

State-Level Initiatives

Collaboration at the state level occurs between state agencies as well as between state agencies and local programs. States are moving forward in sponsoring special projects or initiatives to encourage the development of family literacy programs, and have begun to coordinate cross-agency funding to facilitate such development. As the first state to implement a comprehensive approach to family literacy, Washington instituted a program similar to Even Start in the mid-1980s. In addition, Kentucky has been a leader in supporting the implementation of the four-component model of family literacy, and state officials were active in extending the center-based model programs in North Carolina (Brizius & Foster, 1993).

State support for family literacy has included the passage of legislation on family literacy (e.g., Hawaii, Louisiana, and Arizona), as well as the inclusion of family literacy provisions as part of broader school reform initiatives. In some states, such as Illinois, interagency groups are working together to sponsor family literacy programs. In a current project sponsored by the Lila Wallace-Reader's Digest Fund, the National Center for Family Literacy is working with California, Illinois, New York, and North Carolina to build state infrastructures for family literacy that include a training system for family literacy and interagency state activities to foster the development of local family literacy programs.

Private sector organizations and foundations also are helping to support family literacy through programs such as matching grants. In fact, the William R. Kenan, Jr. Charitable Trust was an early leader in funding model family literacy programs in Kentucky and North Carolina. The Toyota Motor Corporation and the John S. and James L. Knight Foundation continue to support family literacy programs that require matching funds from local communities as well as the participation of local agencies in partnerships for delivering services.

As the funding for education and human services moves entirely toward block grants, the lessons from state initiatives on effective cross-agency collaboration become more critical. However, few of these efforts have been evaluated, pointing to the need for more rigorous studies.

A Preliminary Framework for Family Literacy

An initial step in understanding the conditions that give rise to cross-agency collaboration, as well as the process of developing and sustaining interrelationships in family literacy, is to use a *heuristic device*, such as a framework, for defining the variables of interest and specifying the types of

relationships that might be examined. The classical literature on organizational relationships and social exchange theory provides a point of departure for developing such a framework.

Agencies generally form interrelationships because they are compelled to do so, or because they have a common objective or a mutual need and consider it in their own best interest to work together (Cook, 1977). In the case of family literacy, some legislative mandates or state policy initiatives have called for collaboration by requiring that agencies join together in developing multi-component services. Private sector initiatives in family literacy also have required multi-agency participation in funding and in program development.

In contrast to situations mandating or initiating cross-agency collaboration, agencies may voluntarily work together to fund programs or to enter into other arrangements for exchanging services or information. Under such circumstances, the conditions for collaboration are specified by the participating agencies as a tool for meeting a common need. The activities of local family literacy programs in organizing support services for clients and in carrying out multi-component services are illustrations of this type of collaboration.

Recent research on interagency coordination in adult education (Alamprese, 1994; Alamprese, Brigham & Sivilli, 1992; Alamprese, Schaff, & Brigham, 1987), family literacy and support programs (MacDonald, 1994; Quezada & Nickse, 1993; Kagan, 1991), and job training (Bailis, 1989; Grubb et al., 1989) provides some insight into understanding the factors that are important for developing and sustaining effective collaborations. While these studies have identified similar strategies used by programs to carry out collaborations, the work on adult education coordination also addresses the structural conditions that give rise to organizational interrelationships.

When organizations attempt to work together at both the local and state levels, it appears that two types of collaboration strategies are important—strategies organizations use to develop relationships, and the communication mechanisms that are used to sustain these relationships. As noted in the literature, an initial step that organizations take in developing a collaborative relationship is to determine the benefits and costs of exchanging resources, information, or services. Three factors concerning the perceived benefits and costs of a relationship are important in organizational as well as individual development of relationships. These are: (1) the extent to which the parties involved view the relationship as reciprocal (Gouldner, 1959); (2) the extent to which the benefits of engaging in a relationship are perceived to be at least equal to or more than the costs (Blau, 1964); and (3) the extent to which the benefits are perceived to be proportional to the investment that is made in establishing a relationship (Homans, 1961). In the case of family literacy programs, the agencies involved in designing the services must first determine what they can offer other agencies and what they expect in return. This process where agencies identify the costs and benefits is a critical step in forming a collaborative relationship and should be undertaken by agencies individually before they attempt to work together. When agencies meet, they then must decide whether the payoff from working together in providing services such as adult and early childhood education outweighs the effort that is needed to develop and maintain such services.

Once organizations decide that it is beneficial to all to work together, they must determine the boundaries of their relationship. Organizations use both formal and informal agreements to set boundaries, which often delineate the types and amount of resources that are to be exchanged. Formal agreements usually are needed when fiscal resources or staff are transferred between agencies or programs, while informal agreements are used for other exchanges, such as information, where staff rely on personal knowledge and trust. The available data on family literacy programs indicate that informal arrangements are more likely to be used by the agencies working together in these programs. Almost half of the projects in the Even Start evaluation used informal arrangements, while less than a quarter of the agencies entered into formal agreements (St. Pierre et al., 1993). This pattern of beginning with informal agreements in

establishing collaborative relationships was found in a study of interagency coordination of state and local adult education programs, wherein state agencies, in particular, used informal agreements to test the collaborative process *before* formulating agreements for interagency transfer of funds or other resources (Alamprese, Brigham, & Sivilli, 1992).

Perhaps needless to say, the communication that takes place both between and within organizations has been recognized as an important element in developing and sustaining collaborations. In short, agency staff must develop a common set of goals or a joint vision about what is to be accomplished. Local family literacy planning groups or state and local interagency task forces and advisory councils are mechanisms that programs use to create a mission and to monitor its progress. In the Even Start programs, about a third of the agencies in each of the three service components (adult education, early childhood education, and parenting education) reported the use of an advisory group (St. Pierre et al., 1993). Program staff also use their formal and informal networks in building interorganizational relationships. The annual conferences sponsored by the National Center for Family Literacy have been occasions for network building for program staff at both regional and local levels.

A final aspect of collaboration that is important is leadership, which can come from staff in state agencies or in local programs. At the state level, the sponsors of a family literacy initiative have critical roles in guiding interagency activities, fostering connections with local programs, and providing technical assistance. In addition to providing coordinated funding through the Request for Proposal process that combines funding streams to support family literacy programs, state agencies also can encourage local programs to use set-aside funds to support family literacy activities. Local program collaboratives also need individuals who monitor the progress of a multi-component program and assure that the relationships among the members are balanced. These individuals have critical roles in using mechanisms such as regularly scheduled meetings between agency representatives to discuss aspects of the collaborative that are working and aspects that may need alteration.

Tentative Areas for Research

The components of the framework discussed above provide a starting point for identifying the key research issues that should be addressed concerning cross-agency coordination. Given the lack of research on cross-agency coordination in family literacy, there are a number of areas that would benefit from study. Since most previous research in collaboration has not addressed the structural conditions that lead to successful interagency relationships, it is important to understand the conditions, such as legislative or policy mandates or voluntary actions, which result in effective family literacy programs. The processes that agency staff use to join together in funding or providing services also are not well documented. The family literacy field would benefit from research that examines the processes for assessing the benefits of a relationship; the procedures used in setting relationship boundaries and establishing formal and informal agreements; the mechanisms for communication such as advisory councils and networks; and the strategies that are useful for providing state and local leadership to a collaborative.

The area of inquiry with perhaps the smallest knowledge base is that dealing with direct and indirect outcomes from collaboration. While not an end in itself, cross-agency collaboration can be thought of as an intervening variable that plays an important function in effecting outcomes from family literacy programs. A prior step to studying outcomes is, therefore, to develop a better understanding of the processes used to generate and to sustain cross-agency collaboration. Once the nature of collaboration is documented, it would be useful to examine whether collaboration leads to improved family literacy services or enhanced support for families at the community or state level.

With the solidification of federal funding, the need for effective cross-agency collaboration becomes more important. Since the structure of family literacy services *is* a collaborative process, and

little is known about the effects of that process, any research agenda on family literacy should include studies of collaboration and its disparate consequences.

References

Alamprese, J.A., (1994). Strategies for building collaborative relationships and articulated programs. In *Transitions: Building partnerships between literacy volunteer and adult education programs.* Washington, DC: National Alliance of Business.

Alamprese, J.A., Brigham, N., & Sivilli, J.S. (1992). *Patterns of promise: State and local strategies for improving coordination in adult education programs.* Washington, DC: COSMOS Corporation.

Alamprese, J.A., Schaff, R.L., Brigham, N. (1987). *Project Literacy U.S. (PLUS): Impact of the first year's task forces.* Washington, DC: COSMOS Corporation.

Association for Community Based Education (1993). *Effective practices in community based family literacy: Results of a national research and evaluation project.* Washington, DC.

The Barbara Bush Foundation for Family Literacy (1989). *First teachers*, Washington, DC.

Bailis, L.N. (1989). *An assessment of the JTPA role in state and local coordination activities.* Arlington, VA: James Bell Associates, Inc.

Blau, P.M. (1964). *Exchange and power in social life.* New York, NY: Wiley & Sons.

Brizius, J.A. and Foster, S.A. (1993). *Generation to generation: Realizing the promise of family literacy.* Ypsilanti, MI: High/Scope Press.

Cook, K. (1977). Exchange and power in networks of interorganizational relationships. *Sociological Quarterly,* 18:62-82.

Gouldner, A. (1959). Reciprocity and autonomy in functional theory. In Gross (Ed.), *Symposium on Sociological Theory*, 240-70. New York, NY: Harper & Row.

Grubb, W.N., Brown, C., Kaufman, P. & Lederer, J. (April 1989). *Innovation versus turf: coordination between vocational education*

Job Training Partnership Act programs.
Berkeley, CA: National Center for
Research in Vocational Education.

Homans, G.C. (1961). *Social behavior: Its
elementary forms.* New York, NY:
Harcourt Brace.

Kagan S.L. (1991). *United we stand.* New York,
NY: Teachers College Press.

Kagan, S.L. and Shelley, A. The promise and
problems of family support programs. In
Kagan, S.L., Powell, D.R., Weissbound,
B., and Zugker, E.F. (Eds.) (1987).
*America's family support programs:
Perspectives and prospects.* New Haven,
CT: Yale University Press.

MacDonald, M. (1994). *Reinventing systems:
Collaborations to support families.*
Cambridge, MA: Harvard Family
Research Project.

National Center for Family Literacy (1995).
Family literacy: An overview. Louisville,
KY.

National Center for Family Literacy (1991).
*Toyota Families for Learning progress
report,* Louisville, KY.

National Institute for Literacy (1993). *National
literacy grants program: 1992-1993 Final
report,* Washington, DC.

Nickse, R.S. (1991). *A typology of family and
intergenerational literacy programs:
Implications for evaluation,* paper
presented at the annual meeting of the
American Educational Research
Association, Chicago, IL.

Quezada, S. and Nickse, R. (1993). *Community
collaborations for family literacy.* New
York, NY: Neal Schuman Publishers.

St. Pierre, Swartz, R.J., Murray, S., Langhorst, B.,
and Nickel, P. (1993). *National evaluation
of the Even Start family literacy program:
Second interim report.* Cambridge, MA:
Abt Associates.

Weiss, H.B. (1988). Family support and education
programs: Working through ecological
theories of human development. In H.B.
Weiss, and F.H. Jacobs, (Eds.), *Evaluating
Family Programs.* New York, NY:
Aldine De Gruyter.

English Immigrant Language Learners: Cultural Accommodation and Family Literacy

Richard Durán
University of California – Santa Barbara

The first section of this paper sketches in a broad perspective of the nature of literacy and its intimate connection to the knowledge of cultural practice, institutional practice, and linguistic practice. The subsequent section discusses ways in which literacy acquisition is implicated in the cultural accommodation of immigrant families from non-English backgrounds. The paper then goes on to discuss the importance of research on literacy interventions aiding the cultural adaptation of immigrant families, and the need for research on literacy training interventions that might be used to assist the literacy acquisition and cultural accommodation of families. Comments also are offered regarding the promise of research on use of electronic technologies and computers to improve the literacy of immigrant family members.

> *In trying to understand the nature of literacy and literacy needs among immigrant families . . . we need to have a sound grasp of the full range of cultural, linguistic, and social knowledge that families need to acquire in order to survive. This understanding is not well-served by considering only information provided by formal assessments . . . pertaining to reading, writing, oral comprehension, and speaking skills.*

Literacy Orientation

Viewed in a narrow sense, *literacy* is the ability to comprehend and produce natural language in its written form. A broader definition of literacy encompasses functional notions of literacy tied to the ability to use both written and spoken language to accomplish specific problem-solving and communicative goals arising in the workplace or in conducting transactions within everyday institutions of the community (Venezky, Wagner & Ciliberti, 1990).

This paper pursues a yet broader notion of *literacy*, as that referring to the general semiotic ability of individuals to interpret and to act upon the world within cultural and social communities of practice (see Scribner, 1978, and Wertsch, 1991, for a discussion of relevant perspectives). This broader definition of literacy proposes that there is a fundamental connection between language, communication, and everyday cultural activity. In order to participate in such everyday activities, individuals must interpret the cultural and social demands and contexts of activities, and the means of using language to participate effectively in cultural and social activities. This perspective on literacy emerges from the consideration of the social and cognitive roles language and communication play in people's daily lives. This approach to literacy is especially useful for a better understanding of how community members adapt to social environments involving multiple cultural perspectives and multiple languages.

Scribner and Cole (1981), for example, discuss ways in which Vai tribespeople in West Africa use Vai script, written Arabic, and written English in the pursuit of daily cultural activities. Vai script is used in casual social communication among community members, while Arabic script is read aloud as part of Moslem religious practice. English is used predominantly for formal, government pronouncements and documents. One of the most important contributions of Scribner and Cole's analysis is the indication that communicative competencies in each language are tied intimately to the sociocultural identities and cultural practices

---

of community members. Particular functions such as invitations for family gatherings, reading religious prayers, and communicating laws and edicts, require use of a specific target language, and appropriate discourse forms.

In the context of the United States, Heath (1983), Moll, and others (see papers in Ferdman, Weber & Ramírez, 1994; Saravia-Shore & Arvizu, 1992; Goldman & Trueba, 1987) have examined ways in which the daily cultural activities of ethnic and racial minorities are related to both language practices and socialization involving different varieties of English and different non-English languages. This body of work suggests that acquiring and learning to use one or more languages cannot be separated from learning how to be a competent participant in activities requiring language use.

Defining literacy as "literate action" (Floriani, 1994; Durán & Szymanski, 1995) requires an understanding of how people construct communication and how they interpret everyday situations to pursue social ends. Literate action requires that individuals construct activities as sense-making and goal-achieving endeavors involving the interpretation of culture (Bruner, 1986, 1990).

Research suggests that learners of a second language acquire the second language most effectively when it arises as *comprehensible input* (i.e., when the use of the second language arises in authentic social contexts with extended meaning and uses for practical problem solving) (see papers in Malave & Duquette, 1991; and Krashen, 1981). If we are to help immigrant, non-English background families develop literacy, we must explore how language, culture, and society are intertwined. Furthermore, as will be shown in discussion of the concrete experiences of immigrant family members, we must assess the social and personal needs of family members in a firsthand manner, acknowledging the life perspectives and values of the family, both as a collective whole and in terms of the needs of individual family members.

The work of the sociologist Pierre Bourdieu (1977, 1984) suggests various notions of capital which are helpful in framing relationships between literacy in its expanded sense and social organization, which are particularly relevant to understanding the literacy needs of immigrant individuals and families. Bourdieu proposed that the ability of individuals to participate in everyday activities is governed by a variety of forms of human capital. The phrase cultural-linguistic capital can, therefore, be used to refer to the knowledge embodied in ways of acting and communicating. In order to request assistance from a medical practitioner, for example, an individual needs to know how to act the role of a person seeking medical assistance, and must be able to communicate with medical practitioners based on common beliefs about authority and how to provide information about an ailment. Cultural-linguistic capital is know-how developed through social experience and familiarity with the social, cultural, and linguistic demands of everyday interactions. In addition, again adapting from Bourdieu, one can suggest that social institutions themselves have their own know-how or social capital. While cultural capital is know-how that individuals bring to social institutions, the institutions themselves have know-how that may or may not be fully congruent with the cultural-linguistic capital of individuals. For example, think of the institutional capital of the hospital in terms of knowledge of how to speak and communicate about medical ailments with patients. Further, think about the potential incompatibility which arises when the cultural-linguistic capital of a patient does not allow adequate access to the institutional capital of the hospital. These are the circumstances faced by a non-English background immigrant seeking medical care.

The point here is that in trying to understand the nature of literacy and literacy needs among immigrant families composed of non-English speakers, we need to have a sound grasp of the full range of cultural, linguistic, and social knowledge that families need to acquire in order to survive. This understanding is not well-served by considering only information provided by formal assessments or questionnaires pertaining to the basic reading, writing, oral comprehension, and speaking skills of immigrants. We should go beyond concern for how well immigrants can perform isolated communicative functions.

We should, in fact, utilize better ways of communicating that allow immigrants to act as competent participants in significant cultural and social activities requiring language use. We need to think of literacy acquisition as being a two-way endeavor involving reciprocal relationships between immigrant family members and community institutions. We need to examine the capital of everyday institutions in terms of the cultural-linguistic and social resources that they provide. Ethnographic studies of the survival needs of immigrant families suggest that public and private institutions can be ill-equipped to assist immigrants with vital literacy needs pertaining to health care, social services, banking and commercial exchanges, schooling of children, and other issues.

Examples of Specific Literacy Needs of Immigrant Families That Often Are Not Well Served by Institutions

Not all immigrant families have the same literacy needs. We are well aware that immigrants with extensive formal education, familiarity with English, and economic resources are not at risk in the same ways as immigrant families with limited educational attainment, little knowledge of English, and no financial resources (DaVanzo, Hawes-Dawson, Valdez & Vernez, 1994). Our own ethnographic research among recent Latino immigrant families (García-Ramos & Durán, in preparation) revealed a number of literacy learning needs among families in the domains of access to housing, English language learning, employment, family restructuring, health care, and parental reaction to and involvement in children's schooling.

While these findings are based on case studies of 11 families and cannot be generalized to an entire immigrant community, let alone to an immigrant population, they are suggestive of areas needing further attention in order to better understand how to make literacy training programs more

effective for immigrant, non-English speaking families.

What the findings cited make clear is that understanding the broader literacy needs of families required not only isolated assessment of basic reading and writing skills in English or in Spanish, but attention to the cultural and social knowledge needs of families. Furthermore, poverty, cultural discontinuity, and cultural conflict were found to play important roles in the adaptive strategies shown by families (and to present real challenges to improving the literacy of immigrant families).

In the area of housing, for instance, parents reported difficulty in understanding the cultural and social meaning of terms used in advertisements for apartment housing, lease and rental documents, and oral communication with landlords about housing rules and regulations. A term used in a rental document such as *head of household*, when translated into Spanish, might be taken to denote "eldest and most respected household member" in an extended family household setting, rather than "chief wage earner," thereby illustrating ways in which cultural and social norms might affect coherent communication regarding housing. Moreover, the high costs of leasing and renting led many families to live in crowded conditions. In one instance, a total of nine adults and five children lived in a two-bedroom, one-bathroom apartment in violation of the terms of their lease.

The family in question described how they tried to prevent the apartment manager from noticing that so many people were living in the apartment. This suggests that immigrant families can find themselves acquiring survival strategies that marginalize their acceptance by other community members — people who play a critical role in their survival. The public's concern about the "illegal" status of undocumented immigrants and their perceived over-reliance on public welfare exacerbates this marginalization.

While immigrant families expressed a strong motivation to learn English and to attend classes in English as a second language, many interviewees reported that participation in English classes was made difficult by transportation and child care needs. In one case a parent had to travel five miles to attend an English class three times a week between the hours of 7:30-9:30 p.m. For a time a neighbor drove her to the English class. When the neighbor moved, the parent ceased attending English class because bus transportation to and from the locale in question ceased at 9 p.m. Other family members spoke of feelings of *unwelcomeness* and cultural and social distance while attending English classes. Some reported that they felt ashamed and uneasy when called upon by the teacher in the presence of other students who showed a noticeably greater familiarity with English.

Poor knowledge of English was recognized by family members as a significant impediment to obtaining employment, but knowing how to search for acceptable employment was itself a significant literacy need. Knowledge of job availability required being able to locate employment agencies or public places where job announcements were posted or where casual labor was hired. In the latter situation, there were no formal announcements that a particular gathering place (such as the fence surrounding a downtown parking lot) was a place to find work—yet this venue became known through word of mouth among immigrant community members.

In the case of skilled labor, informants commented on the difficulty they faced in understanding the kinds of work experience and skills needed in order to apply for jobs. Female respondents indicated that they could only find jobs below their skill levels because of lack of knowledge of English. Some indicated that they were forced to accept wages below expected wages in order to retain their jobs. One respondent reported that it was common for immigrant workers to be given virtually no notice about job termination. Another respondent indicated that it was a significant challenge just to learn how to get to a new job via public transportation. Just learning how to read a bus schedule in English and requesting information from a bus driver proved daunting tasks.

Immigrant families with non-English backgrounds also expressed the difficulties they experienced in

their social adjustment to life in the United States: they experienced cultural conflicts with their role in raising children, and a lack of understanding of the role schools play in the socialization of children. The lives of families were changed overnight by moving to the United States. Relationships with kin and community were disrupted, as were culturally valued ways of connecting families to community life. Respondents reported that life in the United States encouraged relaxing or dropping values of *compadrizmo*, wherein families befriend each other and support each other's well-being.

Relationships within families also were transformed. One common complaint of Hispanic immigrant parents was that they found it difficult to discipline their children in a manner which established proper respect between a child and parent based on values in their natal culture (largely Mexican). Parents reported that some of their children threatened to report parents to school authorities if they were corporally punished at home. In turn, these parents felt that discipline at school was too lax and was turning their children against them.

In Mexico, parents were taught not to question the authority of the school, and to trust the social values transmitted through the schools. The perceived tolerance of schools for children's inappropriate behavior was viewed as a violation of cultural expectations and a destabilizing force in maintaining culturally desirable relations within the family.

In addition, many parents reported a lack of understanding of the curriculum encountered by children at school, and about their children's progress in school. Some parents were not aware of low-curriculum tracking of their children, and reported that they were accepting of "satisfactory" grades of students. Participation of Hispanic immigrant families in school parent meetings also proved problematic.

Although Hispanic immigrant children constituted the majority of children at one school, parent meetings were conducted in English with limited input and reaction from parents who were dominant in Spanish. Hispanic parents who needed a translation of meeting proceedings into Spanish sat separated from the other parents. By the time the translator had completed a translation of the preceding comments, the discussion had turned to other topics, thereby making the participation of Spanish-speaking parents difficult.

Some Directions for Literacy Intervention Research

Immigrant, non-English background families living under economically at-risk conditions have cultural-linguistic literacy needs as well as institutional capital literacy needs. We need to explore ways in which agencies providing literacy training can be made more sensitive and accessible to immigrant families. Agencies must acknowledge the existing cultural-linguistic capital possessed by family members, while at the same time assisting families in acquiring new cultural and linguistic capital. We should pursue intensified research on community-based literacy programs serving immigrant families which are dedicated to creating general community consciousness and local public policy awareness of the needs of families in critical domains of sociocultural survival (Fingeret & Danin, 1991). We especially need research on programs and interventions that stress the importance of individuals and families establishing confidence in their own learning and in helping themselves (Wrigley & Guth, 1992).

Research on literacy initiatives supporting biliteracy also should be undertaken. There is strong evidence that the learning of English is a universal and eminently valued goal of immigrants, a goal which is not inconsistent with the desire of families to retain cultural and linguistic ties to their natal cultures (Gillespie, 1994).

Finally, research should examine ways in which electronic technologies can improve the literacy of immigrant families and family members. The emergence of simple-to-use "point and click" computer capabilities has created new forms of cultural-linguistic and institutional capital that are potential tools for promoting literacy acquisition among non-English background immigrants. Children of immigrant families are being given

access to computers at school, and some of the computer software is available in both Spanish and English versions. The World Wide Web has emerged as a new medium of communication augmenting software and videodisks.

Children are gaining access to this new technology at an increasing rate. If for no other reason, the implications of this new medium for children and family members need to be investigated. This new medium spans local, national, and international settings, allowing users to explore knowledge bases that would have otherwise been difficult to access.

Parents' collaboration with children in learning to use electronic technologies seems an especially promising area for research. Making electronic technologies accessible to immigrant families will require research on the design of appropriate institutional systems to permit families' access to technologies. What settings will be most effective for what purposes? Will school computer labs, libraries, and other public institutions prove as viable as home settings for access to technology?

Clearly, poor immigrant families are unlikely to be able to afford purchase of computers, software, video disk players, and phone line equipment necessary for home access to electronic technology. And further, family members' use of technology will be assisted by the availability of suitably trained staff to aid them in the setting where technology becomes available.

References

Bourdieu, P. (1977). Cultural reproduction and social reproduction. In J. Karabel & A. Halsey (Eds.), *Power and ideology in education*, 487-510. Oxford, England: Oxford University Press.

Bourdieu, P. (1984). *Language & symbolic power.* Cambridge, MA: Harvard University Press.

Bruner, J. (1986). *Actual minds, possible worlds.* Cambridge, MA: Harvard University Press.

Bruner, J. (1990). *Acts of meaning.* Cambridge, MA: Harvard University Press.

DaVanzo, J., Hawes-Dawson, J., Valdez, R.B. & Vernez, G. (1994). *Surveying immigrant communities: Policy imperatives and technical challenges.* Santa Monica, CA: RAND, Center for Research on Immigration Policy.

Durán, R. P. & Szymanski, M.H. (1995). Cooperative learning interaction and construction of activity. *Discourse Processes,* 19(1), 149-64.

Ferdman, B.M., Weber, R.M. & Ramirez, A.G. (Eds.) (1994). *Literacy across languages and cultures.* NY: State University of New York Press.

Fingeret, H.A. & Danin, S.T. (1991). *They really put a hurtin' on my brain: Learning in Literacy Volunteers of New York City.* Durham, NC: Literacy South. ERIC Document Reproduction Service, No. ED 332 026.

Floriani, A. (1994). Negotiating what counts: Roles and relationships, texts and contexts, content and meaning. *Linguistics and Education,* 5 (3&4), 241-74.

García-Ramos, R. & Durán, R.P. (In preparation). *Latino immigrant life and literacy needs in cultural and social contexts.*

Gillespie, M.K. (1994). *Native language literacy instruction for adults. Patterns, issues, & promises.* Washington, DC: National Clearinghouse for ESL Literacy Education.

Goldman, S.R. & Trueba, H.T. (Eds.) (1987). *Becoming literate in English as a second language.* Norwood, NJ: Ablex Publishing Corporation.

Heath, S.B. (1983). *Ways with words.* New York: Cambridge University Press.

Krashen S.D. Bilingual education and second language acquisition. In California State Department of Education (Ed.), *Schooling and language minority students: A theoretical framework.* Los Angeles: Evaluation Assessment and Dissemination Center.

Malave, L.M. & Duquette, G. (Eds.) (1991). *Language, culture, and cognition.* Philadelphia: Multilingual Matters.

Saravia-Shore, M. & Arvizu, S.F. (Eds.) (1992). Cross-cultural literacy: *Ethnographies of communication in multiethnic classrooms.* NY: Garland Publishing, Inc.

Scribner, S. & Cole, M. (1981). Unpackaging literacy. In M. F. Whiteman (Ed.), *Writing: The nature, development, and teaching of written communication: Vol 1. Variation in writing: Functional and linguistic-cultural differences,* 71-6. Hillsdale, NJ: Lawrence Erlbaum Associates, Inc.

Scribner, S. (1979). Modes of thinking and ways of speaking: Culture and logic reconsidered. In R.O. Freedle, *Advances in discourse processes: Vol. 2. New directions in discourse processing,* 223-44. Norwood, NJ: Ablex Publishing Corporation.

Venezky, R.L., Wagner, D.A. & Ciliberti, B.S. (Eds.) (1990). *Toward defining literacy.* Newark, DE: International Reading Association.

Wertsch, J.V. (1991). *Voices of the mind: A sociological approach to mediated action.* Cambridge, MA: Harvard University Press.

Wrigley, H.S. & Guth, G.J.A. (1992). *Bringing literacy to life: Issues and options in adult ESL literacy.* San Mateo, CA: Aguirre International.

Designing and Conducting Family Literacy Programs That Account for Racial, Ethnic, Religious, and Other Cultural Differences

Vivian L. Gadsden
University of Pennsylvania

This paper focuses on the issues of race, culture, and class, and their implications for instruction and learning in family literacy programs.[1] However, the discussion presented in the paper reconfigures the question assumed in the title. Rather than asking learners to justify their cultural and social histories, it is presupposed that programs will assume responsibility for seeking out this information as an essential part of program development, and that they can and will pose the issues for themselves. Learners' racial, ethnic, religious, and cultural history cannot be dismissed easily, even when learners choose not to make this history *an issue* in their learning, or when the history or the daily experiences of the learners are dissimilar to those of the instructor or to other learners.

Family and intergenerational literacy programs are among the most rapidly growing educational

> *Rather than conceptualizing the racial, ethnic, and cultural histories of learners as an addendum to design and conduct, programs must assess the strengths and knowledge voids that their staff members bring to the task of teaching and the cultural assets and individual limitations that the populations they serve contribute to the learning environment.*

intervention efforts in the United States. Often appended to federally funded, school-based programs intended to serve low-income families such as Even Start and early childhood programs such as Head Start, family literacy has been integrated into a variety of "life-span" programs that aim to serve adults and children alike (Mikulecky & Lloyd, 1995). However, the

constructs of these programs differ, sometimes dramatically, and researchers and practitioners in other domains (e.g., workplace and adult literacy) argue that it is difficult to see "how to make such programs work," given their varied purposes and the many interpretations of even the *concept* of family literacy.

Family literacy programs, themselves, report that they experience many of the problems faced by other types of literacy programs. However, the specific intergenerational issues embedded in our conceptualization and implementation of family literacy efforts dictate that these programs focus on critical questions of parenting, family support, and reciprocal teaching and learning within and outside of home contexts. Despite this slight deviation in the specific purposes and contexts of family literacy, as a field family literacy and the programs that have emerged over the past few years have not addressed many of the critical and complex issues identified by other programs such as school-based and adult literacy programs. Questions about instructional and curricular development persist, as do problems of retention and the more basic issues of program design, development, and implementation for multiple and diverse populations. Like other literacy efforts, family literacy programs serve populations who share common problems, such as problems of reading and writing and often the attendant problems of poverty, but who sometimes differ greatly in racial, cultural, and religious affiliation; socio-political histories and ethnic connectedness; socio-economic backgrounds; and life views.

The issues of race, class, and culture are central to family literacy and are tied to many of the very purposes for which parents and children from diverse backgrounds enter programs, as well as the real experiences of their daily lives. In my own research, parents connect the issues of race and class to questions of access, and have clear and defined purposes for sustaining their participation in programs (see Gadsden, 1995a and 1995b). The impact of these racial and cultural factors as well as life experiences frame the ways that learners value and use literacy, and the ways in which they come to construct views about the processes involved in literacy learning and program participation.

The first task of existing programs would seem to be to re-examine their own purposes, commit themselves to understanding the social and cultural contexts in which the learners they serve live and develop, and conceptualize learning and teaching as reciprocal processes. This puts programs in a position to collect the different experiences of family members and to recast them into appropriate curricula that engage and motivate family members who participate in programs. As part of the initial step, programs might explore approaches to obtaining information about learners' ethnic and cultural beliefs and practices; assessing the importance of these beliefs and practices to learners' purposes for participating and to their family experiences; and identifying ways that these beliefs and practices can be integrated into the program effectively and appropriately.

This paper is divided into four sections, beginning with an overview of the conceptualizations of family literacy for programs. The focus then shifts to the importance of social and cultural practices within families, and parents' perceptions of family literacy. Next, instructional concerns of race, class, and culture for family literacy are considered. As summary and conclusion, the purposes of family literacy instruction are revisited and the focus is on ways of thinking about the design and development of family literacy efforts that integrate historical, cultural, and racial issues into instruction, and that generate a more global context for family literacy programs.

Conceptualizing Family Literacy

Whether and how practitioners and researchers consider issues of race, class, or culture are largely measures of how they conceptualize the field in

which they work or the goals of that work. A fundamental issue is what family literacy actually means to the establishment and survival of programs themselves, and what it means for those developing instructional and learning activities and the definitions of family literacy that contribute to the program's mission. As in other areas of literacy, family literacy practitioners and researchers may:

- attend to these issues as "add-ons";

- ignore them in favor of a generic, *one-size-fits-all* curriculum; or

- become deeply vested in transforming curricula.

As noted in other places (e.g., Gadsden, 1994), research on family literacy is developed around a variety of themes that attempt to explain the relationship between children's performance in school and parents' literacy levels or literacy practices in the home. Purcell-Gates (1993) identifies four of these themes. One is developed around research findings that suggest children first acquire basic cognitive and linguistic skills within the context of the family. A second theme suggests that substantial literacy learning occurs in the years prior to children's receiving formal instruction. A third describes parents' education and literacy practices in the home as critical to children's school achievement and performance on tests; and a fourth theme stresses the difficulties faced by low-literate parents when they assist their children in literacy learning. Embedded in each one of the themes are cultural identities, histories, and experiences of family members, all of which contribute to whether and how learners become engaged in and sustain learning.

These themes often are discussed within two perspectives on family literacy. One perspective describes literacy as composed essentially of school-based academic activities within family contexts, and assumes that parents—particularly low-literate, low-income parents—want to support their children's literacy development, but lack the knowledge and understanding of school-based strategies and approaches to assist their children to develop the literate behaviors required in classroom settings (see Edwards, 1990). A second perspective highlights the importance of understanding existing family practices as a prerequisite to developing curricula that build upon home and community knowledge and experiences (see Auerbach, 1989). Family practices and interactions are examined to determine the functions, uses, and purposes of literacy within families; and programs are developed around the contextual needs of family members.

Several program models were put into effect over the past ten years, although little, in general, is known about the design of family literacy programs (see Paris et al., 1995). The most widely known of these models include the *Kenan Model* of the National Center for Family Literacy; *Parents as Partners*, developed by Edwards; the Missouri *Parents as Teachers* program, developed by Winter and her colleagues; and the *Home Instruction Program for Preschool Youngsters* (HIPPY). In addition, parent-child reading curricula and on-site programs have been developed by researchers such as Strickland and Morrow (1989), Paratore et al. (1992), and Handel and Goldsmith (1989).

The differences in the structure and content of program models (and in their possible outcomes) appear to be modest in some cases, although the interpretations for practice, stated purposes, or ideological bases of the projects may vary substantially. What is noteworthy, however, is that, although these program models are used disproportionately with families of color and families in low-income homes, and although each model highlights its work with different populations, none specifically addresses issues of racial, class, gender, or cultural differences in discussions centered upon assessment or instructional approaches and strategies. Based upon work done in Michigan, Philadelphia, and other sites throughout the country, many individual programs collapse parts of the above models for their own purposes and attempt to develop culturally responsive curricula (e.g., a Chicago program that uses an Afrocentric approach and a Los Angeles program designed to meet the needs of Mexican-American families).

Cultural and Social Practices of Families

Research studies and data from the field suggest that programs must be mindful of the strengths of families and the cultural communities in which families exist (Ferdman, 1990). Family literacy efforts that do not build on such strengths may succeed for parents and children in the short term, but may fail on a long-term basis, or, at least, will not be sustained. Although strengths have rarely been delineated clearly, the social connectedness of the family to others in the community and with those who share common cultural traditions and interests is often identified as important.

In several studies on families of color, including papers written on immigrant and indigenous groups, researchers describe variability in the approaches to literacy; relationships among parents, children, and other family members; and expectations within the family as a function of culture. All of these often combine into what I call *family cultures*: collections of beliefs, practices, and approaches to which family members contribute and from which they extract, and which are modified over the life-course of the family (Gadsden, 1995a).[2] These family cultures, as I have noted from my research with multiple generations of African American and Puerto Rican families, provide individual family members with a way of constructing their futures within or oppositional to the life-course trajectory of the family. My own research in programs and in different cultural communities reminds me that families wield enormous power in the lives of adult and child learners and a high level of value is attached to cultural traditions and to the problems that families associate with race and racism.

When program staff and practitioners lack knowledge of these familial or cultural traditions or minimize, ignore, or devalue the importance of these factors, their unfamiliarity may be interpreted as a lack of interest or may result in their implementing practices and activities for the program that offend the learners or their families. Jerri Willett and David Bloome (1992), for example, show that over time children began to experience tension, anger, hostility, resistance, and alienation in their relationships at home when their literacy experiences did not enable parents to participate. Concha Delgado-Gaitan (1987) found that Mexican-American parents wanted a better life for their children and were eager to support their children's literacy development, but often used systems of support that did not mirror those of the dominant American culture.

Gail Weinstein-Shr (1991), referring to her work with Cambodian families, focuses on the degree to which the western-centered, time-honored view of history and culture constrains the opportunities for children and parents of other cultures to develop literacy; traditions within families defined children's roles in specific ways. My own work (Gadsden, 1995a) with multiple generations within the same families suggests that in the intergenerational messages within the African American families studied, perceptions of power, powerlessness, and access are inseparable from the value of literacy or the nature of access; parents convey the value of literacy along with a sense of the difficulty in achieving literacy.

While there is relatively little research that examines parents' specific concerns about culturally responsive instruction and materials, Lily Wong-Fillmore's accounts (1990) from Hispanic parents suggest that these parents seek out and value sound early educational programs that are also culturally sensitive. Parents in a Head Start parent literacy project in the National Center on Adult Literacy described literacy in relation to its socially enabling qualities and its role in empowering their children to address societal inequities (Gadsden, 1995b). In another study, parents defined access in specific socially and culturally contextualized ways, stressing the potential impact of literacy for ensuring power and success for future generations (Gadsden, 1995a).

Despite research support for the importance of cultural knowledge and our intuitive sense that issues of race, class, and culture matter, neither family literacy research nor practice typically raises these issues. Some programs may discuss them as separate concerns, cite them in program readings, or examine them in relationship to family members' perceptions, for example,

whether parents and children perceive that literacy can and will make a difference in their lives. Whatever the program's stance, program staff must determine for themselves how to access information and how to translate what is known about culture, ethnicity, race, and gender for family literacy learners. This presumes that the staff will include some people from the cultural and ethnic groups of program participants. However, when this is not the case (and often it is not), programs and the practitioners who are part of the programs will need to evaluate their ability to obtain this information and to create learning environments that do not simply invite participants to offer such information but also respond to what is learned.

The critical questions here are bound to culture and to context: Family literacy practitioners, like other practitioners, enter their classrooms with assumptions and beliefs about their students. Work in family literacy must unravel assumptions and encourage strong learning contexts respectful of the lived experiences and goals of parents, children, and other family learners.

Practical Concerns for Programs

Parents and children who participate in family literacy programs, though disproportionately low-income and families of color, differ within these descriptions and across a variety of other social and cultural dimensions. I often consider these in-group variations and the tendency to hope for a unilinear explanation for the behaviors and experiences of socially less powerful groups. As an African American, I am asked often to respond to questions about the needs of the black community or the problems of black children. The people asking the questions assume that blacks represent a monolithic group with similar experiences, apparently unaware of or neglecting the fact that within this collective, called blacks, there are many different subgroups and cultures, just as there are in other cultural and ethnic groups.

People who consider themselves black Americans may be of continental African, Caribbean, or

African American heritage; they may be native speakers of Spanish, French, English, or different African languages or dialects; or they may share common histories but have different traditions and familial expectations. What most may have in common, however—as is true of Hispanics, Asian Americans, American Indians, and European Americans—is a core of common examples of how others respond to them in school, work, or social settings. That is, black men may be feared; Hispanics, even those who are native-born, may be treated as limited-English-speaking immigrants; Asian American students desperately needing educational support may not receive it because of a perception that they are all good students; and European Americans may be considered racist even when the label does not apply. The point is that racial, cultural, class, and social issues are complex for all people across all ethnic groups—and are not the "natural preserve" of people of color.

How does a family literacy program begin to examine these issues? Programs will need to separate the package of issues by identifying written materials and other resources that help provide a context, and then reassembling the issues with the help of the very populations that they serve—in a way that enables staff, family learners, and the program to learn and grow. If we address issues around race, ethnicity, and culture, for example, we might consider the meaning of these terms and the ways in which we as practitioners, researchers, and learners manipulate these concepts. Historically, curricula in Pre-K–12 and other educational settings present race and culture as unchanging, biological concepts, when in fact our experiences tell us that these concepts are fluid and change as social situations and practices change. In addition, despite the fact that women as mothers are over-represented in family literacy programs, too often issues of gender are excluded from discussions or readings.

A family literacy program begins to deal with issues of diversity by developing activities that encourage learners to examine their own concepts of the terms and by providing readings that provide context for the issues. This process should begin at the first meeting and in assessment activities and should continue throughout the instructional program. Practitioners and learners might share information about their own ethnic, racial, and cultural histories; examine their own family histories and origins; and talk about, write about, and analyze their own experiences. Particularly as we work with parents who have goals around their children's development, the focus on the family's cultural, social, and ethnic histories can be used as a point of entry to conversations about the purposes, uses, and valuing of the literacy learning that is occurring between parent and child.

Family literacy classrooms must be settings in which teachers and students demonstrate mutual respect for the knowledge and experiences that each brings into the classroom, and developed upon the premise that teaching and learning are reciprocal activities: within each teacher, there is a learner, and within each learner, there is a teacher. Issues of race, culture, ethnicity, gender, and religion are difficult to discuss in groups that are diverse and large. I have found that even in my own teaching of university graduate students, the allure of these issues as concepts is more appealing to students than the reality of discussing them. What is important in developing a "space" for this conversation and in developing appropriate curricula for the university course and for work in family literacy programs is to enable students to meet in pairs and small forums. These small groups enable students to speak openly and to engage in a variety of important cognitive activities. To determine the best approach to take and to determine what the most critical and urgent issues are, practitioners must rely on their own observations and invite "feedback" from students.

Considering Difference and Commonality for Teaching and Learning

There is no fool-proof method to assure that programs respond to the expectations of learners. However, this paper suggests ways of thinking about "difference" and "commonality."

As an initial step, programs must assess the resources and the limitations of existing program structures, content, and focus. Rather than conceptualizing the racial, ethnic, and cultural histories of learners as an addendum to design and conduct, programs must assess the strengths and knowledge voids that their staff members bring to the task of teaching—as well as the cultural assets and individual limitations that the populations they serve contribute to the learning environment. Programs must investigate the ways that reading and writing activities build upon both differences and commonalities of families and of the learners within those families. They must encourage learners to see themselves and their familial and social history as critical domains within which literacy develops.

Family literacy programs also must "carve out" their purposes, identifying whether program content will focus on parenting education, job preparation, parent-child interactions, parent-child book reading, or some combination of activities, and the ways in which these foci can be developed to attend to issues of race, culture, class, and gender.

Next, the programs must be explicit and committed to the development of literacy, including notions of reading, writing, computing, and problem-solving. Through activities and exercises that connect reading, writing, cultural issues (including family life), and experiences as integrative, programs can set the stage for learners to connect their multiple selves (e.g., as parents, students, and workers) with the program. In other words, programs signal to learners that it is appropriate and important to include their "cultural selves" in the process of literacy learning. Toward that end, a variety of activities might be used.

In addition, program staff must work with family literacy program participants in engaging their family members in discussions about their emergent literacy skills, in order to help family members understand and support the participants' learning. This not only encourages shared discourses within families but also increases the continuity between the activities of program, home, and other contexts.

Focus on family support requires that family literacy programs specialize in a core of expectations and program demands. Family literacy researchers and practitioners must, then, consider the learner within a context, sometimes as an individual and at other times as a member of a cultural, ethnic, and social collective called the family. Practitioners and family literacy learners can go on to construct portraits of learning and of new self-images that become a part of home and family life and that reflect the personal experiences of parents and children learning together and may, of course, include grandparents, grandchildren, and other family members. However, the value that family members assign to the learning in a literacy program may be affected by the degree to which non-program participants in the family view the time and effort expended by the family literacy learner as intrusive to the daily functioning and experiences of the family. These issues are a part of the fabric of family life and may be revealed publicly by learners or masked as private issues. Practitioners can assist learners by not intruding unnecessarily into their personal lives, but by establishing a range of activities that are "safe places" for learners to explore new ideas and to reconcile their desires for learning with other positive and negative experiences in their lives.

The central actors in family literacy programs are those who learn (and, in many ways, their families) and practitioners. Like families, programs are most effectively supportive when they include an interchange of ideas, trust, and mutual respect, as well as projections for the future course of activities and an expectation that learning will occur through commitment. Practitioners and family literacy learners are co-constructors of the context of teaching, learning, and knowledge generation. To understand where, when, and how positive change can occur requires understanding how learners and families define themselves, particularly when the teacher and student differ substantially in their cultural, social, or ethnic backgrounds.

With less fear of differences, the practitioner can open up the possibility of building on commonalities that are not threats, but rather contributions, to knowledge. The practitioner will need to know, of course, about the learner and his or her family, and the learner should be knowledgeable about the practitioner. Both can use such information as a springboard in co-constructing the course of instruction and learning, realizing hopes and goals, and sharing personal and intellectual power to expand what has been called in historical accounts of African American families, "the power of knowledge (Holt, 1990)."

References

Auerbach, E.R. (1989). Toward a socio-contextual approach to family literacy, *Harvard Educational Review, 59,* 165-87.

Delgado-Gaitan, C. (1987). Mexican adult literacy: New directions for immigrants. In S.R. Goldman & H. Trueba (Eds.), *Becoming literate in English as a second language.* Norwood, NJ: Ablex.

Edwards, P. (1990). *Talking your way to literacy: A program to help non-reading parents prepare their children for reading.* Chicago: Children's Press.

Ferdman, B. (1990). Literacy and cultural identity. *Harvard Educational Review, 60,* 181-204.

Gadsden, V.L. (1994). Understanding family literacy: Conceptual issues facing the field. *Teachers College Record, 96,* 58-86.

Gadsden, V.L. (1995a). Literacy and poverty: Intergenerational issues within African American families. In H. Fitzgerald, B. Lester, & B. Zuckerman (Eds.), *Children of Poverty,* 85-119. New York: Garland.

Gadsden, V.L. (1995b). Representations of literacy: Parents' images in two cultural communities. In L.M. Morrow (Ed.), *Family Literacy: Connections in Schools and Communities,* 287-303. Newark, DE: International Reading Association.

Handel, R., & Goldsmith, E. (1989). Children's literature and adult literacy: Empowerment through intergenerational learning. *Lifelong Learning: An Omnibus of Practice and Research, 12,* 24-27.

Holt, T. (1990). Knowledge is Power: The Black Struggle for Literacy. In A.A. Lunsford, H. Moglan, & J.S. Levin (Eds.), *The Right to Literacy.* New York: Modern Language Associations.

Mikulecky, L. & Lloyd, P. (1995, May). *Parent-child interactions in family literacy programs.* A paper presented at the National Center for Family Literacy Conference, Louisville, KY.

National Center for Family Literacy. (1993, September). *The NCFL Newsletter.* Louisville, KY: National Center for Family Literacy.

Paratore, J. (1992, December). An investigation of the effects of an intergenerational approach to literacy on the literacy behaviors of adults and on the practice of family literacy. Paper presented at the annual meeting of the National Reading Conference. San Antonio, TX.

Paris, S.G., Gadsden, V.L., Parecki, A. & Edelin, K. (1995). *Family literacy: Characteristics of exemplary programs in Michigan.* NCAL Technical Report. Philadelphia, PA: University of Pennsylvania, National Center on Adult Literacy.

Purcell-Gates, V. (1993). Issues for family literacy research: Voices from the trenches. *Language Arts, 70,* 671-77.

Strickland, D. & Morrow, L. (1989). Creating curriculum: An emergent literacy perspective. *The Reading Teacher, 42,* 722-23.

Taylor, D. & Dorsey-Gaines, C. (1988). *Growing up literate: Learning from inner-city families.* Portsmouth, NH: Heinemann.

Weinstein-Shr, G. (1991, April). *Literacy and second language learners: A family agenda.* Paper presented at the annual meeting of the American Educational Research Association, Chicago, IL.

Willett, J. & Bloome, D. (1992). Literacy, language, school, and community: A community-centered view. In A. Carrasquilo & C. Hedley (Eds.), *Whole language and the bilingual learner,* 35-57. Norwood, NJ: Ablex.

Winter, M. & Rouse, J. (1990). Fostering intergenerational literacy: The Missouri Parents as Teachers Program. *The Reading Teacher, 43,* 382-86.

Wong-Filmore, L. (1990). *Latino families and schools.* Unpublished manuscript.

Endnotes

[1]Issues of gender are particularly important to discussions in family literacy. I have included only modest references to gender and to religious differences because both issues deserve wider attention than is possible in this analysis and are included in the references to culture as a broad concept.

[2]In recent work, I have developed a framework called "family cultures" which combines developmental context of families with life-course issues.

Family Literacy Programs: Creating a Fit with Families of Children with Disabilities

Beth Harry
University of Miami

Families with children with special needs can be expected to have more than their fair share of challenges, not the least of which is learning to adapt to their children's disabilities. This paper focuses on what is known about this type of adaptation, and how such knowledge can be helpful to literacy interventionists. One caveat, however, should be noted at this point: although the terms *adaptation* and *coping* are used throughout this paper, it should not be assumed that families of children with disabilities necessarily see the challenges presented by their children as problems that have to be *coped* with. Many parents have commented that this is a negative framing of something all families must do: confront whatever challenges life brings.

This paper begins with a brief summary of the main and most current research-identified issues on family coping strategies. Second, the need for any intervention program to establish a "fit" with the coping styles of the family will be considered. Third, trends in research on family literacy that suggest effective directions for interventionists—in particular, with families of low-income minority status—will be identified.

> *The most important question . . . is how interventionists can design programs that will not add to the challenges faced by the family, nor disrupt the adaptive process already established by the family . . . . (I)nterventionists must know what families actually do on a day-to-day basis, and must identify the existing beliefs and skills of family members regarding literacy.*

Research on Families' Adaptive Strategies

Interventionists who wish to have a positive impact on family literacy should be aware of the coping strategies families are likely to engage in as they respond to the needs of a child with a disability. Indeed, they should be aware that, over the years, research on the issue of stress has shifted its focus from stressors to coping strategies, as it has become clear that many families exhibit a surprisingly high level of *salutogenesis* (sense of well-being), rather than pathology (Antonovsky, 1993). This is not to deny, however, that many families do become overwhelmed by the crisis (Singer, 1993).

A considerable body of research has sought to identify the factors that determine how stressful a child's disability will be to the family, as well as the kinds of supports that may alleviate that stress. A review by Shea and Bauer (1991) summarizes the main determinants as:

- parental traits;
- the nature of the child's exceptionality;
- care-giving demands of the child;
- internal social supports;
- external social supports;
- financial resources; and
- family constellation and relationships.

A source of stress noted more recently (Beckman, 1994) is the efforts of service providers and intervention programs, their good intentions notwithstanding.

Hill's *ABCX* family crisis model (1949) and recent adaptations (McCubbin & McCubbin, 1987) have been useful in sorting out the process of adaptation to potentially stressful events. The A, B, and C aspects of the model refer, respectively, to the stressful event, the family's personal and material resources for responding to it, and the meaning or interpretation the family places on the event; the confluence of these three factors determines X—the nature of the outcome for the family.

While early research tended to focus on the A and B factors (such as the nature of the child's exceptionality and the resources of the family), more recent approaches have attended to the C factor—with the belief that the meaning family members attribute to the event is a crucial factor in their adaptive process. One approach to understanding the C factor is to try to identify the *cognitive coping* strategies used by parents. Turnbull and Turnbull (1993) define cognitive coping as "thinking about a particular situation in ways that enhance a sense of well-being" (p. 1). Researchers who have pursued this concept have based their work on cognitive adaptive theory, which holds that personal adjustment includes resolution of "a search for meaning," "an attempt to gain mastery," and "enhancing self-esteem" (Behr & Murphy, 1993; Affleck & Tennen, 1993).

From a practical point of view, the most important question for this paper is how interventionists can design programs that will not add to the challenges faced by the family, nor disrupt the adaptive process already established by the family. To ensure that these negatives are not present, interventionists must know what families actually do on a day-to-day basis, and must identify the existing beliefs and skills of family members regarding literacy. Affleck and Tennen (1993) recommend that researchers seek to establish a much greater "descriptive base," and recommend that this be sought through the use of "intensive time sampling studies of the daily lives of individuals" (p. 145).

In a recent line of research, the team of Gallimore and colleagues at the University of California, Los Angeles, investigated the ways parents construct what they call the family's *ecocultural* niche. This research offers detailed documentation of the types of accommodations parents make to their daily routines, in response to the needs of the child with the disability (Bernheimer, Gallimore & Kaufman, 1993). Not unlike earlier research on care-taking demands (Beckman, 1983), one dominant finding of this research is that children with high medical and behavioral needs tend to require greater parental accommodations to their daily routines than do children with mild or severe developmental delays. Such research should form the base of intervention designs, so as to create a fit between the design and the family. As Bernheimer et al. (1993) state: "Interventions that are fitted to the existing daily routine [of the family] appear to be more sustainable" (p. 266); therefore, researchers should "design interventions that capitalize on existing daily routines and ecocultural features [rather] than to attempt to create new activity slots" (p. 266).

Knowledge has been limited partly because it has been focused on subjects that, typically, are white and middle-class (as noted by Behr & Murphy, 1993)—in part because such families, it is argued, are easier to access through service agencies, and partly because these are the families who are, it seems, better able to respond to the formal questionnaire methods traditionally used by such research. It is important to access the views of families who do not belong to the dominant cultural groups in the society, partly because the incidence of disability is increasingly disproportionately high among these groups (U.S. Department of Education, 1992), and because our knowledge is simply too limited without their views. For example, research suggesting that some minority groups may show greater resilience when faced with disability is sparse but strong (Marion & McCaslin, 1979; Vasquez, 1973; Mary, 1990; Hanline & Daley, 1992).

The research methodology, then, is important both in determining the types of data that can be collected and the demographics of the sample likely to be accessed. With the advent of Public Law 99-457 and the increasing call for family centered services in early intervention, the need for naturalistic and qualitative methods is becoming increasingly evident. In the naturalistic paradigm, the view of knowledge acquisition as a dynamic, interactive process allows the researcher to document not only what families' attitudes and practices are, but why they exist, and how they change over time. The personal approach of the naturalistic researcher, who, it is often observed, replaces the traditional *research instrument* (Peshkin, 1988), allows for the gradual development of trust and rapport, through which parents may become comfortable enough to reveal concerns and attitudes that would easily be missed by one-shot, paper and pencil investigations (Daley, 1992). This is particularly true for lower socio-economic groups—those populations typically missed by these methods—and especially for minority groups who, historically, have had considerable reasons for not trusting representatives of society's mainstream.

Another aspect of traditional survey methodology is that a structured questionnaire can only elicit responses to the questions asked, and is, therefore, very much influenced by the underlying premises of the researcher. More open-ended approaches have the capability to find out how the subjects define the issues, rather than mirroring the assumptions of the researcher. This is not to deny that more personalized approaches are also open to bias and require a rigorous self-awareness on the part of the researcher (Peshkin, 1988; Harry, in press).

Creating a Fit with the Adaptations Families Have Made to Disability

In applying the foregoing discussion to the question of family literacy interventions, it is suggested the two central challenges are:

- how to ensure that the intervention will be a help and not a hindrance to the family; and

- how to design an intervention that respects and builds on families' beliefs and skills regarding literacy.

As pertains to the first challenge, interventionists must begin by taking into account the likelihood

that any formal intervention might create even more stress for the family. There is the stress of having one more set of people to deal with; the stress of having one more activity to do; the stress of having to account to one more person for what you did or did not do; and the stress that results from fearing that your own attempts as well as the intervention may not be successful—that you might, in effect, be a failure one more time.

On the positive side: there is the hope that one more person in your life might help to relieve your stress; that one more activity might be just the thing that will create a long-awaited improvement for your child or family; the reward of receiving approbation for your efforts from someone you respect; and the reward of achieving success for your child, your family, and yourself.

The interventionist who faces these possibilities in planning will do well to begin by gaining a detailed picture of the family's daily life: what are the daily routines of the home, and what is the impact of the child with special needs on those routines? What is the social style of the family? As suggested earlier, Goldenberg, Reese, and Gallimore (1992) have demonstrated the effectiveness of the concept of *activity settings* as a means of gaining such information. They define activity settings as "the concrete and observable manifestations of leading cultural activities" (p. 500). The researchers collect information on five aspects of the daily activities of families: "the personnel present and available for participation; the cultural goals, values, beliefs, and attitudes that the participants bring to the activity; the immediate motives, purposes, emotions, and intentions guiding the action; the nature of the tasks that are accomplished; and the scripts, normative behaviors, and patterns of appropriate conduct used during the activity" (p. 501). Such information will inform the researcher as to what is likely to fit comfortably into the family schedule. Concerns about fitting into a family's daily schedule are closely tied to my second question—how to fit a design to the family's belief system about literacy. It is not hard to see that an approach that does not fit with the family's beliefs is more likely to create stress and less likely to be successful.

Creating a Fit with Families' Beliefs and Practices Regarding Literacy

In our increasingly diverse society, with its widening gap between rich and poor, literacy interventions for families are focused on those with children most at risk of school failure—poor and minority children. Researchers concerned with including parents in the development of children's literacy continue to be concerned with an evident discrepancy between the theories of academics and the folk theories and cultural styles of low-income, language minority, and ethnic minority families. As summarized by Goldenberg, Reese, and Gallimore (1992): literacy specialists focus on "meaning based and communicatively based activities with print," while parents interpret literacy as "learning and mastering the orthographic code" (p. 529).

Several studies vividly illustrate this finding (Daisey & Murray, 1991; Delpit, 1988; Goldenberg, Reese & Gallimore, 1992; McLane & McNamee, 1990; Harry, Allen & McLaughlin, in press; Stipek et al., 1992). The studies also strongly suggest that parents' education and/or socio-economic level are the important determinants of these beliefs, rather than culture or ethnicity per se.

Goldenberg et al. (1992) concluded their discussion of the *dilemma* facing family literacy interventionists with the statement that there are two choices—either to train parents in the desired intervention, or to adapt the intervention to the skills and beliefs of the family. They argue for the latter. "Our intervention plans must be informed by parents' understandings no less than by our own, presumably more scientific ones" (p. 530). Similarly, on the same issue, Delpit (1990) argued that "educators must open themselves to, and allow themselves to be affected by, these alternative voices" (p. 100).

A dual approach could be argued for, particularly one that starts with the parents' skills and knowledge and aims to add to parents' repertoires, as appropriate. This approach takes into account both a respect for parents' views and the belief that parents can learn new strategies (Delgado-Gaitan, 1992). Beliefs about how children learn are perhaps closely tied to child rearing philosophies, and like those philosophies, will not be changed by precept, only by experience. *To start where the parents are* means that parents will be afforded an opportunity to experience success in helping their children. Indeed, since decoding skills are an essential part of learning to read, why should parents' theories be denigrated? Why shouldn't more meaning-based approaches be introduced as additives to, rather than replacements for, what parents already do?

Goldenberg's study observed that parents were comfortable with a more *playful* literacy style when they perceived an activity as being a conversational, non-school activity. The view that oral and written traditions are separate, and that the latter belongs to schools, should not be surprising when we note that many minority groups have come from cultures that hold a strong tradition of oral as opposed to written literacy. It seems very likely that parents who see progress in their children's reading and writing can be made aware of the link between oral and written traditions, and will not be averse to increasing their repertoire of literacy activities with their children. Thus, I concur with the conclusion of Goldenberg et al. (1992):

The house of literacy has many rooms, and each room that is constructed makes a contribution to the edifice. Learning letters and sounds and how they combine to form words is a very important part of literacy development, along with reading and talking about whole texts, pretending to read and write, and so on... (p. 530).

It is strongly recommended that family literacy interventions utilize open-ended designs requiring a detailed knowledge of the kinds of adaptations made by families of children with special needs; and further, that the interventions be based on information about families' beliefs and practices regarding literacy. Designs may begin with a phase of ethnographically detailing such aspects of family functioning—and move on to an intervention that fits into the family's activity settings and that builds on parents' existing skills and beliefs. The open-ended design will allow for modifications to the intervention in response to an ongoing evaluation of the projects' success.

References

Affleck, G. & Tennen, H. (1993). In A. P. Turnbull & H.R. Turnbull (Eds.), *Cognitive coping, families, and disability*, 135-50. Baltimore: Brookes.

Antonovsky, A. (1993). The implications of salutogenesis: An outsider's view. In A.P. Turnbull & H.R. Turnbull (Eds.), *Cognitive coping, families, and disability*, 11-122. Baltimore: Brookes.

Beckman, P.J. (1983). Influence of selected child characteristics on stress in families of handicapped infants. *American Journal of Mental Deficiency*, 88(2), 150-56.

Beckman, P.J. (in press). The service system and its effects on families: An ecological perspective.

Behr, S.K. & Murphy, D.L. (1993). In A.P. Turnbull & H.R. Turnbull (Eds.), *Cognitive coping, families, and disability*, 1151-164. Baltimore: Brookes.

Bernheimer, L.P., Gallimore, R. & Kaufman, S.Z. (1993). Clinical child assessment in a family context: A four-group typology of family experiences with young children with developmental delays. *Journal of Early Intervention*, 17(3), 253-68.

Daley, K. (1992). The fit between qualitative research and characteristics of families. In J.F. Gilgun, K. Daley & G. Handel (Eds.), *Qualitative methods in family research*, 3-11. Newbury Park: Sage.

Daisey, P. & Murray, A. (1991). Parents and teachers: A comparison of perceptions and attitudes toward literacy growth. Paper presented at the New Directions in Child and Family Research: Shaping Head Start in the Nineties, Arlington, VA.

Delgado-Gaitan, C. (1990). *Literacy for empowerment*. New York: Falmer.

Delpit, L. (1990). The silenced dialogue: Power and pedagogy in educating other people's children. In N.M. Hidalgo, C.L. McDowell, and E.V. Siddle (Eds.), *Facing racism in education*, 84-102. Cambridge, MA: Harvard Educational Review.

Goldenberg, C., Reese, L. & Gallimore, R. (1992). Effects of literacy materials from school on Latino children's home experiences and early reading achievement. *American Journal of Education*, 100, 497-537.

Hanline, M.F. & Daley, S.E. (1992). Family coping strategies and strengths in Hispanic, African-American, and Caucasian families of young children. *Topics in Early Childhood*, 12(3), 351-66.

Harry, B., Allen, N. & McLaughlin, M. (in press). "Old fashioned, good teachers": African American parents' views of effective early instruction. *Learning disabilities: Research and practice*.

Hill, R. (1949). *Families under stress*. New York: Harper & Row.

Marion, R.L. & McCaslin, T. (1979). *Parent counseling of minority parents in a genetic setting*. Unpublished manuscript, University of Texas, Austin.

Mary, N.L. (1990). Reactions of Black, Hispanic, and White mothers to having a child with handicaps. *Mental Retardation*, 28(1), 1-5.

McCubbin, H.I. & McCubbin, M.A. (1987). Family stress theory and assessment: The T-Double ABCX model of family adjustments and adaptation. In H.I. McCubbin & J.I. Thompson (Eds.), *Family assessment inventories for research and practice*, (3-34). Madison, WI: University of Wisconsin, Madison.

McLane, J. & McNamee, G. (1990). *Early literacy*. Cambridge, MA: Harvard University Press.

Peshkin, A.R. (1988). In search of subjectivity - one's own. *Educational Researcher*, 17, 17-22.

Shea, T.M. & Bauer, A.M. (1991). *Parents and teachers of children with exceptionalities*. Boston: Allyn & Bacon.

Turnbull, A.P. & Turnbull, H.R. (Eds.) (1993). *Cognitive coping, families, and disability*. Baltimore: Brookes.

Singer, G. (1993). When it's not so easy to change your mind. In A.P. Turnbull & H.R. Turnbull (Eds.), *Cognitive coping, families, and disability*, 207-20. Baltimore: Brookes.

Stipek, D., Milburn, S., Galluzzo, D. & Daniels, D. (1992). Parents' beliefs about appropriate education for young children. *Journal of Applied Developmental Psychology.*

U.S. Department of Education, Office of Special Education Programs. (1992). *A report of the National Longitudinal Transition Study of special education students.* Menlo Park, CA: SRI International.

Vasquez, A.M. (1973). *Race and culture variables in the acceptance-rejection attitudes of parents of mentally retarded children in the lower socioeconomic class.* Unpublished doctoral dissertation, California School of Professional Psychology, Los Angeles.

Longitudinal Study of Family Literacy Program Outcomes

Andrew Hayes
University of North Carolina at Wilmington

The question, "Are family literacy programs effective?" has no simple answer, although American society often demands simple answers to complex questions. To approach the real complexity logically, one must discover for whom literacy programs are effective and under what conditions effectiveness is assured. To be effective, itself, this paper will begin by defining conceptual terms used throughout, including

- evaluation,

- research, and

- family literacy.

In addition to discussing the above terms and the ideas that give them meaning, some conclusions shall be drawn concerning target families, program operations, and program effects that have implications for evaluation and research design (as well as for data interpretation).

> *When compared to General Educational Development (GED) production, job placements, or other direct adult-education goals, family literacy programs may show less effects than single-service programs. The cumulative effects on the family are expected to be greater in the long term for the family literacy programs, however.*

Evaluation

Many definitions of *evaluation* exist, but the one most useful for guiding planning and action is: *The processes for providing information for choosing among alternatives in the task of decision-making* (Stufflebeam et al., 1971).

A concept that is central to this definition is another term, *information*, which, as used here, refers to data that have the capability to reduce the probability of error in a choice among alternatives. Thus, by definition, information is useful for the intended decision-making function; and, to be sound, evaluation designs must reflect directly any decisions to be made, including who will make them and how they will be made.

Research

It seems reasonable that a definition of *research* should be useful for directing the planning and conducting of a project. For definition, research includes all processes through which information is provided for reducing the probability of error in reaching conclusions regarding the object of the research itself.

Family Literacy

Several recent publications have addressed the question of how to define family literacy (Brizius & Foster, 1993; Harris & Hodges 1995; Morrow, 1995; Morrow, Tracey, & Maxwell, 1995; Morrow, Paratore, & Tracey, 1994; and Tracey, 1995). All studies have indicated the need for such a definition, and some have attempted to fill that need, with different degrees of success. Most attempts, however, have done little to define the concept in terms that could support planning for inquiry to determine changes in *family literacy*.

To serve the need for planning evaluations or research projects, the definition here focuses on *literate families* only. This working definition was arrived at by determining the capabilities needed by family members to ". . .communicate expectations of accomplishment to their children," as only one example. The list of capabilities below were derived directly from the several general family characteristics that are considered central to providing a setting or a context that would have *desired* intergenerational effects be present.

The literate family capability areas seem to be those needed to assure a setting and family conditions that can suffice to support development and learning by children within the family context. Each of these items, when considered alone, seems to be necessary but not sufficient for supporting family development. Furthermore, evidence of change in only one, or a small number, of these items does not indicate that a change in family literacy has occurred, even though the change that did occur may be important to individual members or, for that matter, the whole family. In short, each of these items identifies an area of capability that can be assessed for evaluation of program effects or for research. The definition here used for a literate family is made up of many parts, including the ability or means to

- acquire needed or desired information from printed verbal, symbolic, and graphic materials;

- acquire needed or desired information from oral communications;

- communicate their intent or ideas to others in printed (written) verbal, oral verbal, graphic, or symbolic forms;

- communicate the value and worth of actions and being of self and family members;

- communicate in oral and written forms with content in the traditional academic area at a level needed for family tasks;

- judge the plausibility of data in print, oral, or graphic forms;

- judge the plausibility of goals for self and family;

- set short-term and long-term goals for self and family;

- communicate goals to family members;

- make plans for accomplishment of personal and family goals;

- implement plans for accomplishment of personal or family goals;

- analyze problematic situations, and select and manage solutions to problems for self or family;

- make valid predictions of the probable effects of their actions or of family conditions on themselves and others;

- make valid judgments of the perceptions others hold of their own behaviors or ways of being;

- make valid judgments of the quality of their own work and conditions;

- set and communicate expectations for self and others;

- support the development of family members, and help others in the family with their learning and development; and

- acquire skills needed to make changes in self or family that may be needed or desired.

In any given family or target group, the level of attainment of capabilities at the time of enrollment or at any later time may range from full in all areas to substantial deficits in all, or most areas. Literacy needs, therefore, are *any* deficits in the individual or family capabilities listed above.

In a further attempt to produce definitions to support evaluation and research design, *family literacy programs* are distinguished from any of the variety of *single-service* programs available for adults or children. That being the case, family literacy programs are those intervention systems that

- address one or more of the capabilities required for a literate family;

- share intergenerational program goals with the family; and

- provide or coordinate services to meet family literacy needs in a way that is *sufficient* to produce intergenerational effects.

Conclusions Reached and Assumptions Used for Evaluation and Research Design

In programs designed to address long-term and intergenerational changes in lives or capabilities of families, the intervention usually produces direct effects that are attainable during relatively short time periods, and in the same categories as those produced by many programs designed to produce *only* direct, short-term effects. For example, adult-education programs or work-place literacy programs and family literacy programs may produce changes in the education levels of the adults in a family or lead to some form of certification of skill or achievement, but family literacy programs are designed to provide a more complex set of services for adults and children than are programs designed to provide one primary service. The different programs, then, should be expected to have different direct and long-term effects.

While direct, short-term effects of interventions may be of significant value in themselves, for programs designed to produce long-term or intergenerational effects, those effects are *instrumental* to family changes that may require a long period of time to be manifested—more time, in fact, than duration of their participation in a program. The multiple services with long-term goals included in such programs may cause them to be less *efficient* in producing direct, short-term effects than programs with single, direct-effect goals. Thus, when compared on General Educational Development (GED) production, job placements, or other *direct* adult-education goals, family literacy programs *may* show less effects than single-service programs. However, it is expected

that the combined effects of the family literacy program services will be greater in the long term than in single-service systems.

Because of the traditional short-term funding patterns and political decision time frames for special programs, care must be taken in program design and operation to make legitimate the goals of both long-term or intergenerational intervention and short-term indicators of changes in the family context or family culture, particularly those that are *causally* related to conditions in the lives of the children as they grow into adulthood. Without this care, the programs with long-term and family effect goals may *lose out* compared to single-service or single-member intervention programs and services.

Some Points to Consider in Framing Expectations for Long-term Program Effects

The points made in this section describe factors that need to be considered in both setting long-term goals and planning evaluation or research projects. These ideas deal with a variety of factors, some of which have implications for methods, some for variable selection, and some for interpretation of results. Numbered not necessarily according to impact, the points are:

1. Correlational studies (as opposed to causal studies), reported in various professional publications and often quoted glibly in the popular press, have led to many overly simple conclusions about ways to intervene in order to address literacy as well as other conditions of society. While these findings are not incorrect, all are significantly inadequate for framing public policy or for reaching conclusions about causal influences. Yet each finding has been used as a major rationale for direct intervention. Among these findings are:

    - Reading material in the home is related to reading performance.

- Education levels of parents are related to a child's later academic success.

- The amount of time parents spend reading to their children is related to the later academic performance of those children.

- The amount of time that children spend watching TV is related negatively to reading and academic performance.

- Children of single-parent families perform less well than children from two-parent families.

All of these correlational studies and their conclusions suffer from what is considered to be a fatal flaw—*inappropriate variables* were identified by the studies. The variables actually identified are *symptomatic* of the *causal* variables, but *are not* the causal variables, themselves. In all cases, elements of the "family culture" are the *causal* factors; and those cultural elements are revealed by, or manifested in, the behaviors or conditions that were studied. However, the manifestations, or symptoms, were *described* as the causes and thus assumed by many program planners and advocates *to be* the causes.

There is little reason to believe that introducing any one of these conditions into family settings through intervention will have the same effects as when they are present in the family context as a result of their having been introduced into the family as a normal and natural action by the family.

2. The adults who currently comprise a major portion of the U.S.'s undereducated class represent families with histories of undereduca-tion, underclass identity, poverty, and so on. Those characteristics are part of the system of meaning of the families—part of the family culture. Significant changes in these families through external intervention probably will not occur without significant changes in the system of meaning experienced by members. To be effective, interventions

expecting to change that culturally-based system of meaning must be as complex, intensive, and of such duration as is needed by the particular target families to make significant changes.

3. Even under the worst of social conditions and from the most unfavorable family contexts, a large proportion of children turn out OK. Conversely, even under the best of conditions and the most favorable family cultures, many children do not.

4. A large proportion of adults who enroll in family literacy programs had unhappy school experiences. Even if they consider *education* to be important, they may not think of schools as good places to be. Adult programs that are primarily academic in nature, or which are delivered in settings other than schools, often do little to change the view of K–12 schools and schooling that is based on their prior experiences as a student in those schools.

5. Adult-education programs designed primarily to prepare for GED or other *equivalency* certification *can* cause changes with intergenera-tional effects on the lives of families. Whether or not those effects occur depends, of course, upon conditions within the family and upon changes adults make in the family context as a result of their own education.

6. Existing academically oriented adult education programs are not effective for large percentages of the undereducated adults in society. A large proportion (perhaps well over 50 percent) of those persons who enroll do not remain in the various programs, and a large proportion who remain make little or no significant changes in their life states after participation. Data on changes and lasting effects generally are weak.

7. The set of adults who enroll in family literacy programs is not homogeneous. The range of academic functioning at the time of enrollment may be from minimal literacy to near passage of certification exams, or

Designing and Conducting Longitudinal Evaluation or Research Projects

beyond. Families vary, too, according to degree of acceptance of social norms, commitment to change, hopefulness in self and personal conditions, confidence of change, personal capability to learn and change, and supportiveness of their environment. Both short- and long-term family conditions and effects are different among these groups, so there should be different expectations of both short- and long-term effects.

8. Before the age of three or four the cognitive and behavioral patterns of children reflect conditions and values of the home setting. Intervention with the family can cause patterns of behavior to change and can cause expressions of worth and value made by parents and children to change; but even by this early age, the interventions must counter significant patterns of behavior.

9. The social maturity of a large proportion of adults who enroll in family-literacy programs is delayed. In dealing with matters of life, how to solve personal and family problems, and in talking about the future, those adults demonstrate behaviors, views, and values that are similar to those of children during their early-adolescent years. Expectations for types and levels of short- and long-term changes must reflect those levels of adult social maturity.

10. A significantly large proportion of parents who enroll in family literacy programs show little initial understanding of their roles as parents, and especially the role of teacher.

11. Almost all *preschool-age* children enrolling in family literacy programs enjoy attending school, and enjoy being in school with their parents, but many (especially boys) seem to value school attendance during that age primarily because it represents their being "grown up."

It should be clear from the sections above that if longitudinal studies of family literacy program effects and conditions are being considered, some decisions apparently can be based on the information produced. When the question about decisions to be made is raised, however, the responses are either: "We just want to know whether the programs are effective," or "We want to be able to make a case with (whatever the funding agent) so that funding will continue or increase."

Both of these responses are suspect as justification for longitudinal study projects for a variety of reasons that should be apparent from the presentation above. Furthermore, these reasons do not provide the evaluators or researchers with the information needed to design and conduct the project.

"We just want to know" is neither a decision nor a question. If this statement actually means, "To what extent did we achieve some particular objectives?" then the decisions to be made or questions that might be answered with that information need to be identified and made explicit to the sponsors and investigators. As an example, some different decisions that might be based on this information are ones related to program changes, target-audience changes, or changes in the priorities of the organization. These, and other classes of decisions, would require *different* information from the study. Thus, the decisions to be supported must be made explicit at the time of design to prevent either under- or over-production of information and under- or over-allocation of resources.

"We want to get continued, or expanded funding" as a rationale for longitudinal studies generally ignores common processes and rationales for much of public policy decision-making. We often hear about the objectivity and rationality of public policy decision-making as a justification for project evaluations, but my experiences during over 30 years of planning and evaluation work in almost all states, several federal agencies, and in many communities indicate much the opposite. While there certainly are many important exceptions, the basis for decision and action is much more likely to be advocacy, incidental and anecdotal evidence, case presentation, political agendas, value systems, or general perceptions than *objective* evidence of program effectiveness or efficiency. Furthermore, it is unusual for policy decisions to be delayed until the longitudinal evidence is available.

What, then, are some reasons for longitudinal studies of family-literacy program effects? That question must be answered before engaging in the processes themselves.

Conditions Required for Justification of Longitudinal Evaluation or Research

Before the question of long-term effects is addressed for making decisions or answering questions, there are some standards of another type that should be considered to determine whether longitudinal studies can be justified. These are all matters that should be determined as a result of evaluation and monitoring during the operational period or in the short term afterwards, including:

1. There must be some defined and documented target audience for the program, and that audience must have some demonstrated need for assistance that can be served by the program as it was designed.

2. There must be some known (documented) program that the subjects actually experienced.

3. The design of the program or project must be consistent with sound theoretical principles for changing the attributes of families that are identified for change. The design should specify, among other things, what changes are expected to occur, the assumptions about what causes those changes to occur, and the rationale for the designed experiences as vehicles for the intended changes. If the design

makes little or no sense theoretically as a way to bring about the intended changes, or if the intensity or duration of the experiences are inadequate to cause the changes desired, then there can be little justification for allocation of resources to longitudinal studies of effects.

4. There should be some important question or questions that need to be answered about the program effects for which answers are not adequately available in existing literature or obtainable from short-term studies. If sound theoretical and technical information bases exist in literature for making the decisions in project and program design, there is little need to try to *prove* the validity of the theoretical or technical frameworks by documenting the outcomes of their application. If, on the other hand, the model designs are based on hypotheses of causes-and-effects, such studies *may* be justified. If there are sound principles supporting the designs, *accountability* decisions may only require evidence of implementation as designed. If more evidence is needed, comparison of short-term effects with those predicted may be useful.

5. There should be ample evidence that the designed model was the actual program implemented, or that the program actually implemented was documented to such an extent that it can be tested for theoretical validity and then used to explain effects and their conditions.

6. Any short-term effects that are believed to be *necessary conditions* for long-term changes must have occurred to the degree essential to expect the long-term effects to follow. Short-term evidence must support claims that direct, short-term effects actually occurred of the form and to the extent required by the model used to explain how long-term effects occur.

7. Some decisions or questions of enough consequence for justification of the resources required should be explicit and known by the sponsor and investigators. The particular questions to be answered, or criterion-information needs should be known to them.

8. Data bases documenting variations in model implementation among sites and years of operation, and documenting the individual participants and their short-term accomplishments must be available in a form that can be used by the investigators.

9. The identities of the participants and some information about how to contact them must be available in a form that can be provided to the investigators.

10. Relationships with participants that support ongoing contact with them, and that support gathering information from and about them, should have been established during the time of their participation.

11. Resources, including money and technical capability required to obtain information of the forms, quantity, and quality needed, should be available.

Dangers of Longitudinal Studies of Family Literacy Program Effects

If family literacy program models have valid designs and are effective when implemented well, and if evaluation or research projects are important, then it is essential that the information produced by the investigation provide evidence of the validity of the model and of its outcomes.

Data obtained about program effects and conditions leading to those effects are subject to any of a variety of measurement tools, design, and execution problems. There are many well-documented forms of data error that may indicate that programs were not effective or did not function as hypothesized, when, in fact, they were or did function well. Longitudinal evaluation or research projects should not begin unless planners are confident in the design of the project. Among the processes that may, however, produce no-win outcomes are the following:

1. Comparing small groups of family literacy participants in "comparable" groups who participate in other programs, or some who are in no program at all. The differences among the participants within given family literacy programs generally are so great that group statistics—average values, for example—may be inappropriate to use for interpretation or comparison. Direct, statistical comparisons with almost any groups are likely to be suspect because of non-equivalence, whether the results are positive or negative in respect to the question or purpose intended.

2. Using *effects* variables that are likely to be affected significantly by factors other than ones that are under control of the participants, or using ones that are situationally inappropriate. Counting the jobs obtained by people who were formerly on welfare may not reflect the changes—for better or for worse—of the general economic conditions or job market in an area. Counting enrollment in other education programs, or entry into the job market might be misleading for the many women who have young children at home, and are staying at home to care for them until they enter kindergarten.

3. Using tests or other measuring devices that are subject to errors because of *social desirability* or any of several other forms of error; especially if the data are used as if the errors did not occur. All forms of measurement or methods of data-collection are subject to various forms of error, even such forms as interviewing or observing behaviors. All measurement and data-collection materials and processes must be as free of these known forms of error as reasonable to expect in the design.

4. Conducting economic-impact analyses and reporting data in aggregate form as if the conditions and effects for all families served are similar. While data in this form tends to be "sexy," easy to quote, and "headline ready," when presented they are almost always gross overstatements of effectiveness.

5. Identifying the wrong variables —symptoms of, and not the actual interest—or identifying an inadequate set of variables to explain changes or lack thereof, to study and document. Any research relating to intergenerational effects which is for purposes other than hypothesis-development or prediction should address causal variables which help us understand the systems of meaning comprising the culture of homes, and the variable set must be of enough size to comprise a sufficient set to explain variance in effects or conditions. Continuing to address correlations between life states and symptoms or manifestations of social contexts is distracting to the fields of practice.

6. Planning the project for time periods that are either too short or too long to be optimum for providing the information needed.

7. Setting expectations of program effects that are too high (or too low), and then expecting the longitudinal study to document these effects as if they actually *should* occur. (Nickse, 1993).

8. Failing to specify clear purposes for the evaluation or research project.

9. Using inquiry processes that either have significant intervention effects or that create significant barriers to data gathering and follow-up. For example, using participants in data collection is an *unnatural* activity for the family, and would be a form of continuing intervention; and asking participants to keep records of their activities may be both a significant intervention and barrier to their continued participation in the longitudinal study.

10. Using *amount of time enrolled in the program* as a factor related to program outcome. This variable can have little meaning as a factor indicating effectiveness of programs without accounting for all of a variety of variables on which the participants are different, including, among others, entry educational level and capability, goal aspirations, or supportiveness of environment.

Some Purposes for Longitudinal Study

It may seem that the sections above are suggesting that there is little reason to do any longitudinal evaluations or research. Perhaps in a way they are. However, it is wise to remember that evaluation must provide information for decision-making, and research is to provide information that makes answering questions less prone to error. If there are important decisions or questions that probably will be based on the forms of data that can be provided only by longitudinal study, then such studies are essential. If, on the other hand, decisions or conclusions are not going to be based on such information, then resources should be saved—including organizational energy.

For family literacy programs and their related target audiences, there are many unanswered questions about needs, techniques of intervention, systems of services, differences among audiences that justify differences in programs and techniques, and interactions of interventions with other societal factors or systems. These questions may be important to staffs and other decision makers within particular program sites, or within the field in general.

If longitudinal studies are primarily to serve research purposes, they should be justified and designed toward that end. Quite often, research information must take a different form from evaluation information, especially if the decisions to be made are concerned primarily with policy or advocacy. Whatever the form, both the level of informative detail and the form such detail takes will differ significantly.

Some Approaches for Longitudinal Study

It should be clear from the above that there can be no best plan or design for longitudinal study, for the design will always depend upon the purpose to be served. Some approaches to evaluation or research that may fit the information needs for the different conditions are illustrated below. These might be combined in many ways, or modified to fit situations that are different.

1. Start the longitudinal study at the time of planning the family literacy project and the short-term evaluation. Plan to produce a base-line data set that can justify attributing later conditions to program effects or conditions and can demonstrate, also, that changes actually have occurred.

2. Use case-documentation data systems that are designed to allow all appropriate aggregation of case data, including a full range of objective and subjective data. Begin case documentation at the time the subjects are identified, and continue throughout program participation and longitudinal study.

3. For projects with one, or only a few sites, base evaluation studies on case methods, using some system to classify cases into categories that are reasonably related to goals, needs, and family conditions. Interpret short- and long-term effects by category.

4. Document the variations in model implementation each year (or for each client cohort), and plan to consider any significant variations in the interpretations of data.

5. For projects with multiple sites, use a system of best- and worst-case analysis in which participating families are selected from among the sites. These would be the cases we might all agree are "the ones that *really* worked or didn't work". Use investigative methods traditional in epidemiological studies to determine the reasons for success or failure. These cases may be identified at any time in their history with the project at which success or failure can be established, and should be followed as long as useful. The cases can be selected from among the types identified in #3 above.

6. Use staff from a local site who were especially successful in establishing relationships with participants to maintain the client-locator component of the longitudinal study, and use periodic group or individual interviews with site staff to obtain any information they have about former participants.

7. To determine how children perform in schools, use a system in which current teachers are interviewed in person or by telephone. In this process, ask the teacher to provide information about two students—the one of interest, and one selected randomly by picking a number in the range between one (1) and the highest number of students likely to be on a class roll. This second child provides a randomly selected comparison group, giving a *normal* referent. Furthermore, it provides a way to control for social desirability distortions in the responses made by the teachers.

8. Use deliberate sampling methods to select small sets of families who will be the object of intensive case study. These samples may be by family type (#3 above), success stories, or any other useful types, such as representative of a population for which there are some particular interests.

9. At each contact point, obtain as much situational data for the families as feasible to provide foundations for interpretations of later conditions.

Summary

Longitudinal studies of families who participate in family literacy programs should be purposive in nature, and should reflect the variety of technical and theoretical information available about families, political and professional decision-making processes and criteria, cultural and social phenomena and their potential for change, and information-systems design and operation. The varieties of needs, goals, and family conditions among the participants should be used deliberately as factors in data analyses and interpretations; and this variance should not be perceived merely as a problem to be solved by ignoring it or trying to work around it because of its problematic nature.

Studies should be grounded in a sound theoretical design of the program model, which is the object of question, documentation of model implementation, documentation of the short-term effects of model implementation, and documentation of the cases to be studied. Longitudinal studies, after all, require too many resources and too much organizational energy to be conducted in any way but to obtain effects of the highest possible quality.

There seems to be little question at this point in the history of the field of family literacy, however, that several compelling questions *must* be answered through longitudinal study to provide needed focus to the field, to support policy action, to make program-design decisions, and to resist the attacks of critics or others who would use the field as a strategy to gain support for their own interests. Since family literacy program goals are long-term and intergenerational, there are several significant needs for information about how, and to what extent, those goals are, or can be achieved. It will become more difficult over time to advocate for family literacy programs without evidence that important and long-term goals are being achieved by given target populations through family literacy programs that are not being achieved through other intervention systems.

References

Brizius, J.A. & Foster, S.A. (1993). *Generation to generation: Realizing the promise of family literacy.* Ypsilanti, MI: High/Scope Press.

Harris, T.L. & Hodges, R.E. (Eds.) (1995). *The literacy dictionary: A vocabulary of reading and writing.* Newark, DE: International Reading Association.

Morrow, L.M., Paratore, J.R. & Tracey, D.H. (1994). *Family literacy: New perspectives, new opportunities.* Newark, DE: International Reading Association.

Morrow, L.M. (Ed.) (1995). *Family literacy: Connections in schools and communities.*
Newark, DE: International Reading Association.

Morrow, L.M., Tracey, D.H. & Maxwell, C.M. (Eds.) (1995). *A survey of family literacy in the United States.* Newark, DE: International Reading Association.

Nickse, R. (1993). *A typology of family and intergenerational literacy programs: Implications for evaluation.* ERIC Document Reproduction Service No. ED 362 766.

Stufflebeam, D.L. et al. (PDK National Study Committee on Evaluation) (1971). *Educational evaluation and decision making.* Itasca, IL: F.E. Peacock Publishers, Inc.

Tracey, D.H. (in press). *Family literacy: Overview and synthesis of an ERIC search.* Yearbook of The National Reading Conference. NRC.

Family Literacy: Parent and Child Interactions

Larry Mikulecky
Indiana University—Bloomington

The relationship between children's literacy and children's interactions with their parents has long been recognized as significant. A growing body of research on how parents and children deal with literacy, language, and schools in general reveals a tapestry of complex interrelationships. Dozens of research studies reveal that approaches to changing parent-child literacy interactions are generally successful. Studies also reveal that simple interventions are of limited success and that it is very difficult to bring about change that transfers to improved literacy in the home.

Aspects of Parent-Child Interactions

Research over the past two decades has established several aspects of parent-child interactions associated with children's later literacy success. Among these are:

> *Parent-child interactions are important to a child's developing literacy abilities. It is becoming increasingly clear that these interactions involve a good deal more than simply reading to children and providing them with books . . . . (A) growing body of research indicates that the way in which a parent speaks with a child may have as much or more to do with later reading achievement of the child than actual time spent reading to the child.*

- parental reading to and with children;

- complexity of language and strategy used between parents and children;

- parental conceptions of the roles of education and literacy; and

- literacy modeling and support present in the home environment.

Parental Reading to and with Children

Research from the 1970s and 1980s consistently identifies and reports strong correlations between parental reading to and with children and children's later success with literacy (Chomsky, 1972; Laosa, 1982; Anderson et al., 1985; Teale & Sulzby, 1986). More recent research has attempted to identify the essential nature of what transpires during parent-child reading times to make them so beneficial. Lancy and Bergin (1992) found children who are more fluent and positive about reading came from parent-child pairs who viewed reading as fun, kept stories moving with a "semantic" rather than a "decoding" orientation, and encouraged questions and humor while reading. Tracey and Young (1994) studied the home reading of accelerated and at-risk readers and their college-educated mothers. They found no difference in the frequency of children's oral reading during first grade and, indeed, found at-risk readers to actually do more oral reading in second and third grade than did accelerated readers. Tracey (1995), in a later analysis of video-taped reading sessions with accelerated and at-risk readers, notes striking differences in the degree to which the accelerated reader received more physical and verbal attention, support, and extended oral feedback. In a more in-depth study of more than 40 families, Baker, Sonnenschein, Serpell, Fernandez-Fein and Scher (1994) analyzed differences between literacy activities of low- and middle-income families.

Low-income parents reported doing more reading practice and homework (e.g., flashcards, letter-practice) with their kindergarten age children than did middle-income parents; and middle-income parents reported only slightly more joint book reading with their children than did low-income families. These middle-income parents did, however, report a good deal more play with print and more independent reading by children. The nature of what transpires during reading time appears to matter a good deal—perhaps more than the mere fact that parent-child reading occurs.

Complexity of Language and Strategy Use

For more than a decade, Snow and her colleagues have been examining the role of language use by parents and children during reading and in other family activities such as dinner-time conversations and explanatory talk (Snow & Goldfield, 1983; Snow, Barnes, Chandler, Goodman & Hemphill, 1991; Beals, 1992; Beals & De Temple, 1992). This body of work indicates that explanatory talk during mealtimes, and to some extent during reading, plays a greater role in predicting children's later reading achievement in school and on tests than does simply reading to children. Further, the aspect of explanatory talk which seems most relevant are non-immediate or non-literal comments such as those associated with predictions, elaborations, and linking new ideas to previous experiences. An example of such comments is the parent who encourages a child to orally compare a caterpillar's cocoon to the child's sleeping bag while reading a children's book about caterpillars and then further asking for predictions of what the child thinks will happen next.

Lancy, Draper and Boyce (1989) describe the parents of good readers as using expansionist strategies which included graduated support or scaffolding as children attempted to understand stories as well as strategies for avoiding frustration. The parent might begin the story and do much of the talking in the form of modeling the making of predictions. Over time the parent speaks less and

encourages the child to take a more active role in reading or telling the story. This is easier with books read multiple times. If children experience great difficulty, the parents of good readers would help with the difficulty or perhaps make a joke. Parents of poor readers are described by Lancy et al. as using reductionist strategies which focus upon decoding, focused criticism, and sometimes even covering pictures to avoid a child's "cheating" in figuring out a word. The tone is one of reading as a serious job which the child must work to master.

Parental Conceptions of Education and Literacy

Differences in reading behaviors and strategy use cited above suggest that there might also be differences in how parents conceive of education and literacy. It is not true that low-income parents do not value education. Several researchers have reported the high value placed upon education by many low-income families. Delgado-Gaitan (1987) reports that obtaining a better education for children is a major reason given for Hispanic immigration to the United States. Taylor and Dorsey-Gaines (1988), in detailed studies of low-income families whose children succeed in school, report extraordinary sacrifices and efforts being made to support children's education—even when parental education levels were quite low. Fitzgerald, Spiegel and Cunningham (1991), in a study of low- and high-income parents, report low-income parents rating the value of education higher than did high-income parents.

Differing literacy behaviors, however, suggest that there may be significant differences in how parents who value education conceive of literacy. Goldenberg, Reese and Gallimore (1992) report that low-income Hispanic parents mainly emphasize letter naming and spelling-sound correspondences when trying to help their children. Baker et al. (1994), cited above, note that when low-income parents spend time with children, they are much more likely to emphasize explicit instruction as well as the work and practice aspects of literacy. Middle-income parents tend to use stories for entertainment, playing, and extended conversation starters. Literacy is presented and modeled as an enjoyable way to entertain one's self and to understand the world. The work of Lancy and colleagues (cited above) tends to confirm these differences in literacy perception and practice.

Baker, Serpell, and Sonnenschein (1995) note that parent-child literacy relationships are *bi-directional*. That is, children influence parents and are influenced by them. Similarly, a child who finds literacy learning a painful experience is likely to avoid books and to make the reading experience painful for the parent involved. A child who learns to enjoy reading and to see it as an entertainment is likely to ask for books, seek attention while reading, and begin to read more independently. Data reported by Baker et al. support this bi-directional explanation of differing literacy perceptions and practices.

Literacy Support in the Home Environment

There is some disagreement about the role of parental support for literacy in the home environment. Research from the 1970s and early 1980s reported by Anderson et al. (1985) identified more books, magazines, and educational literacy materials in the homes of higher-income families and the families of children who performed well in school. When some researchers have expanded the definition of literacy materials to include more functional materials like notes, bills, grocery lists and so forth, the differences between groups are reported to shrink (Delgado-Gaitan, 1987; Diaz, Moll & Mehan, 1986; and Taylor & Dorsey-Gaines, 1988). Heath (1983) reported that low-income families used literacy, but in a different fashion and for different purposes than did middle-income families. She suggests that the schools, rather than the families, need to change to accommodate to these differences and not focus merely upon middle class literacy use. More recent work (Purcell-Gates, 1994) has provided somewhat contradictory evidence, indicating a low level of print use in low-income homes with the greatest proportion being for daily routines and employing simple language at the clause and phrase level.

Interpretations of evidence for other sorts of parental literacy support also conflict. Low-income parents model less book and magazine reading and tend to take children to libraries less than do higher-income parents (Fitzgerald, Spiegel & Cunningham, 1991; Baker et al., 1994). On the other hand, low-income parents are reported sometimes to make extended use of such literacy-related behaviors as storytelling and singing, as well as making sacrifices to financially and physically support children's education (Heath, 1983; Taylor & Dorsey-Gaines, 1988; Baker et al., 1994; Gadsden, 1995). Again, the professional debate revolves around the meaning of these differences in literacy support and the degree to which schools focus only on the sort of literacy found in middle-class homes.

Interventions in Parent-Child Interactions

Edwards (1995, p. 56) indicates that her work since the late 1980s has consistently documented the desire of low-income parents to learn more about what to do when reading to their children. Typical comments from interviews include the following:

- *I don't know what to do when I open the book. I mean I don't know what to do first, second, third, and so on.*

- *I wish somebody would tell me what to do because I am fed up with teachers saying: "Read to your child."*

Tracey (1995), citing the work of Topping (1986) and others, notes that experimental studies to teach parents strategies to help their children with reading have been largely successful to the extent that parents have learned the strategies. Some parents have learned to increase wait time before correcting children's reading errors; others have learned to offer more praise or to use more contextual prompts as opposed to only word-level prompts. Still others have learned to read storybooks to children using dramatic conventions. Evidence of transfer of learning to home practice and continued use is much more rare. Many of these earlier studies can be seen as single approaches to improved family literacy.

Several more comprehensive family literacy programs began to make their appearance during the late 1980s and early 1990s. These more comprehensive programs tend to include multiple components such as adult literacy education, parent education and support, children's literacy education, and time for parents and children to be together. Examples of such programs include multi-city efforts such as the national Even Start programs funded by the federal government (St. Pierre, Swartz, Gamse, Murray, Decky, & Nickel, in press) and the Kenan model programs supported by the National Center for Family Literacy (Brizius & Foster, 1993; Potts & Paul, 1995) as well as several dozen state and local level programs documented by Morrow, Tracey and Maxwell (1995).

Program Results

Even Start was begun by the U.S. Department of Education in 1989, and is designed to provide literacy training for parents while assisting children in reaching their full potential as learners. The program is designed for parents of children eight years and younger, who are, themselves, over 16 years of age, not enrolled in secondary school, and weak in basic skills. Programs must provide integrated services to accomplish program goals. There is a good deal of variation in how goals are accomplished. By the summer of 1994, Even Start was serving more than 26,000 families in approximately 474 projects (McKee & Rhett, 1995). Evaluation data, thus far, indicate a positive effect on the likelihood of parents obtaining General Educational Development (GED) credentials. Other positive results are less clear. Parental literacy gains are apparent only when programs are able to retain adults in classes for a significant period of time. Parental literacy gains are not associated with children's school readiness scores or with literacy skills. No effects upon parents' attitudes or behaviors related to parenting were detected.

The National Center for Family Literacy has advocated an integrated model of family literacy

instruction for nearly a decade, and has developed a system for providing training and support for instructors and program developers. Brizius and Foster (1993), and Potts and Paul (1995) describe in detail the complex integration of program components. Programs have been particularly successful in maintaining program involvement of clients for approximately 30 hours per week for six or more months leading to documented adult literacy gains and better than expected performance of program children upon entering school.

Mikulecky and Lloyd (1995) have evaluated the impact of programs in five cities upon parent-child literacy-related interactions. After approximately six months in programs (100-120 hours of parent and parent-child together time), significant gains are documented in parent-child home reading, visits to libraries, literacy materials in the home, and children's literacy activities. Children's reported reading of books and magazines increased by 60 percent to more than once a day, and the number of times children scribbled, printed, or made letters increased by 30 percent. Parent book reading with children increased by nearly 70 percent to about once a day and library trips doubled to once every two to three weeks.

The programs studied had less impact in positively influencing parental home literacy modeling and how parents read to their children. Parents did report doing more of their own school work at home, but reported no change in leisure reading patterns. Even though the programs all stressed the importance of play and conversation as integral to children's literacy growth, success in this area was mixed. On rating questions, parents made significant gains in recognizing the important role of play and conversation in developing children's literacy and learning. At the same time, several parents volunteered information about increased use with their four-year-olds of flashcards, workbooks from grocery stores, and worksheets borrowed from older siblings. (None of these activities was suggested by programs and, indeed, ran counter to the approach taken by most instructors). The theme of "literacy as work," which is documented in the work cited earlier in this paper (i.e., Baker et al. and Lancy et al.), was also noticeable among participants in

Kenan model programs even though program efforts focused upon expanded conceptions of literacy. Playing with print, scribbling, talking, and reading increased, but so too did flashcards, worksheets, and workbooks.

Morrow, Tracey and Maxwell (1995) summarize the results of several dozen family literacy programs. The reported results are consistently positive—and results range from positive attitude change to follow-up reports of children's success in school to increased parental participation in school-related events. Only a few programs were able to report on literacy gains and changes in parent-child interactions. One particularly well-documented study (Neuman & Gallagher, 1994; Neuman, 1995) examines young mothers participating in a special family literacy program. Literacy-related play settings were created in the homes of six young mothers who were coached in ways to interact with their children while using literacy related props such as several children's books as well as a toy post-office and toy grocery store.

Mothers were coached in how to orally label objects and in how to focus their child's attention. In addition, they were taught to create special learning situations for their children and ways to coach and converse with them. This procedure is described by Neuman and Gallagher (1994, p. 398) as "fine-tuning parental assistance." The researchers found significant improvement in the areas addressed by their coaching, though these gains declined during the transfer and maintenance portions of the study. They advocate this sort of coaching for parental literacy much like Lamaze coaching for pregnant women or La Leche coaching for breast feeding.

Conflicting Viewpoints

This paper earlier discussed the professional debate over the roles of parental support for children's literacy among middle- and low-income parents. A similar debate exists on the role of family literacy programs. Some researchers and family literacy program designers suggest directly addressing established aspects of parent-child literacy interactions by supplementing literacy

materials in the home and directly teaching parents literacy and language strategies associated with children's literacy success. Auerbach (1995) and others term this approach a "deficit" model because it assumes family deficits which must be remediated. These researchers suggest a deficit approach may undermine existing family strengths while convincing parents they must become people they are unlikely ever to become.

These researchers recommend, instead, what they term a "wealth" model which identifies and connects literacy instruction to existing parental strengths and immediate social concerns. Auerbach (1995) suggests that parents in such programs might learn literacy dealing with such issues as immigration, employment, housing, safety, and drugs. Other researchers (see Edwards above) report that many parents want to know how to help their children with literacy, and resent not being shown explicit strategies for reading with their children.

The issue of what to teach about parent-child interactions can become an especially difficult problem in programs where instructors are middle-income women whose ethnic and cultural backgrounds differ from those of their students. It is one thing to model ways to read a book to a child. It becomes a much larger and more complicated undertaking to suggest that a parent also change her style of dinner conversation and other parenting behaviors such as the very way she explains the world to a child. Furthermore, the concept of reading as fun may be utterly foreign to an adult who has had a decade or more of negative experiences with print and schools. It becomes very difficult to avoid transmitting the false message that the students must abandon nearly all of who they are and become as much like the instructor as possible. One of the attractions of the "wealth" model is that it manages to avoid difficulties by asserting that it is not necessary for programs to influence parent-child interactions.

On the other hand, research over the last decade indicates that parent-child interactions are very important. Theories of how language and literacy develop have been examined, tested, and refined. The relationships between a child's developing literacy and adult literacy modeling, oral explanations, and forms of reinforcement are relationships that go well beyond mere correlations. To avoid the possibility of growth in these areas rather than risk the label of "deficit" seems ill advised. This is especially true since there is evidence that programs can help learners make gains in these areas.

Results from family literacy program evaluations such as those cited earlier document the effectiveness of programs in increasing library visits, materials in the home, the incidence of parental reading to children, and children's literacy-related activity. With extensive interventions, it is even possible to influence and fine tune the manner in which parents interact with their children. Transfer beyond program walls and maintaining what has been learned have been less clearly documented, however.

The sparse, existing evidence suggests programs may require extensive efforts from highly trained instructors to change parental literacy modeling, complex language use, and conceptions of how literacy is learned. Indeed, evidence from several studies suggests simply urging parents to read to children or help with homework may lead to many imitating what is identified as poor and counter-productive teaching practice. Even so, a few long-term studies indicate a positive impact of family literacy program involvement in children's early school success. Data on the impact of pure "wealth" model programs or "empowerment" programs which build curriculum around empowering parents to deal with daily social problems are not yet generally available.

A Middle Ground

A middle ground may be possible. Powell (1995) indicates that long-term discussion groups have proven to be much more powerful tools than direct instruction approaches in changing parenting beliefs and practices. Such discussion groups are usually anchored in dealing with a specific child and specific problems. Often, learning interpersonal relationship skills, which may be new to the young parent, are central to this process. In addition, these groups start by

building upon the parent's current understandings of how to parent.

Howard Miller, an Even Start Project Director, suggests that trust and timing are also part of the mix. Miller (1995) observes:

If you tell me that the way my momma raised me was wrong, I'm probably not going to listen to you. If I learn to trust you and find other things you tell me to be useful, I just might think about what you have to say about raising children.

The power is in the hands of the learner to try new ideas, not in the hands of the instructor to inculcate them.

National Center for Family Literacy model family literacy programs have opportunity for parental discussion groups and trust-building available in the *Parent-Time* component of programs. In addition, Sharon Darling of NCFL indicates that program integration can help with parent-child interactions. For example, one program schedules instruction so that parents preparing for the GED examination learn about wind and the operation of wind upon kites and airplane wings. During the same time period, as part of *Parent-Child Together Time*, parents build and fly kites with their youngsters. Parents are encouraged to share their new knowledge and explain kites. In this way, elaborated use of language and explanation occurs more naturally as parents become more capable of explaining the world. Gadsden (1995) suggests still other activities in which parents and older children can engage in joint projects such as translation of oral histories into written texts, joint study of family or community histories, and genealogical analyses. Such tasks would offer opportunity for extended language use as well as development of interpersonal skills.

Conclusion

Parent-child interactions are important to a child's developing literacy abilities. It is becoming increasingly clear that these interactions involve a good deal more than simply reading to children and providing them with books. In fact, there is some evidence to suggest that simply telling a parent to read to a child may lead to quite different behaviors depending upon the background of the parent. Some of these behaviors may even be counter-productive. In addition, a growing body of research indicates that the way in which a parent speaks with a child may have as much or more to do with later reading achievement of the child than actual time spent reading to the child.

Educators disagree about what is to be done with this information. Some suggest that the information be ignored, since it implies low-income parents may in some way be deficient. It is better to focus upon literacy instruction designed to give parents more control over their world. If this is done, all else will follow. Others point to successes in teaching literacy and parenting strategies to new parents and point out that many parents want to know how to improve the literacy of their children.

A middle ground is possible, but only if the issue of parent-child interactions is addressed with a good deal of sensitivity, tact, and respect for all concerned. Rather than directly teaching new ways for parents and children to interact with language and literacy, an interactive approach involves generating opportunities for discussion, modeling, and practice—as well as time, energy, and talent.

References

Anderson, R.C., Hiebert, E.H., Scott, J.A. & Wilkinson, I. (1985). Becoming a nation of readers: The report of the Commission on Reading. Washington, DC: The National Institute of Education.

Auerbach, E.R. (1995). Which way for family literacy: Intervention or empowerment. In L. Morrow (Ed.), *Family literacy: connections in schools and communities*, 11-28. Newark, DE: International Reading Association.

Baker, L., Sonnenschein, S. Serpell, R., Fernandez-Fein, S. & Scher, D. (1994). *Contexts of emergent literacy: Everyday home experiences of urban prekindergarten children.* (Research report.) Athens, GA: National Reading Research Center, University of Georgia and University of Maryland.

Baker, L., Serpell, R. & Sonnenschein, S. (1995). Opportunities for literacy learning in homes of urban preschoolers. In L. Morrow (Ed.), *Family literacy: Connections in schools and communities* 236-52. Newark, DE: International Reading Association.

Beals, D.E. (1992). Explanation as co-constructed discourse: A study of conversations in low-income families of pre-schoolers. Paper presented at the annual meeting of the American Educational Research Association, San Francisco, CA, April 20-24, 1992.

Beals, D.E. & De Temple, J.F. (1992). Home contributions to early language and literacy development. Paper presented at the annual meeting of the National Reading Conference (42nd, San Antonio, TX, December 2-5, 1992.)

Brizius, J.A. & Foster, S.A. (1993). *Generation to generation: Realizing the promise of family literacy.* Ypsilanti, MI: High/Scope Press.

Chomsky, C. (1972). Stages in language development and reading exposure. *Harvard Educational Review*, 42, 1-33.

Delgado-Gaitan, C. (1987). Mexican adult literacy: New directions for immigrants. In S.R. Goldman & K. Trueba (Eds.), *Becoming literate in English as a second language*, 9-32. Norwood, NJ: Ablex.

Diaz, S., Moll, L. & Mehan, K. (1986). Socio-cultural resources in instruction: A context-specific approach. In *Beyond Language: Social and cultural factors in schooling language minority children*, 87-229. Los Angeles, CA: California State Department of Education and California State University.

Edwards, P.A. (1995). Combining parents' and teachers' thoughts about storybook reading at home and school. In L. Morrow (Ed.), *Family literacy: Connections in schools and communities*, 54-69. Newark, DE: International Reading Association.

Fitzgerald, J., Spiegel, D. L. & Cunningham, J.W. (1991). The relationship between parental literacy level and perceptions of emergent literacy. *Journal of Reading Behavior, 13*(2), 191-212.

Gadsden, V. (1995). Representations of literacy: Parents' images in two cultural communities. In L. Morrow (Ed.) *Family literacy: Connections in schools and communities*, 287-303. Newark, DE: International Reading Association.

Heath, S.B. (1983). *Ways with words.* Cambridge, UK: Cambridge University Press.

Lancy, D.F., Draper, K.D. & Boyce, G. (1989). Parental influence on children's acquisition of reading. *Contemporary Issues in Reading, 4*(1), 83-93.

Lancy, D.F. & Bergin, C. (1992). The role of parents in supporting beginning reading. Paper presented at the annual meeting of the American Educational Research Association, San Francisco, CA, April 20, 1992.

Laosa, L.M. (1982). School, occupation, culture and family: The impact of parental schooling on the parent-child relationship. *Journal of Educational Psychology, 74*(6), 791-827.

McKee, P.A. & Rhett, N. (1995). The Even Start family literacy program. In L. Morrow (Ed.), *Family literacy: Connections in schools and communities*, 155-66. Newark, DE: International Reading Association.

Mikulecky, L. & Lloyd, P. (1995). Parent-child interactions in family literacy programs. A paper presented at the National Center for Family Literacy conference, Louisville, KY, May 20, 1995.

Miller, H. (1995). Comments made at Research Design Symposium on Family Literacy, U.S. Department of Education, Office of Educational Research and Improvement, Washington, DC, Sept. 7-8, 1995.

Morrow, L.M., Tracey, D.H. & Maxwell, C.M. (Eds.) (1995). *A survey of family literacy.* Newark, DE: International Reading Association.

Neuman, S.B. & Gallagher, P. (1994). Joining together in literacy learning: Teenage mothers and children. *Reading Research Quarterly, 29*(4), 382-401.

Neuman, S.B. (1995). Enhancing adolescent mothers' guided participation in literacy. In L. Morrow (Ed.), *Family literacy: Connections in schools and communities*, 104-14. Newark, DE: International Reading Association.

Potts, M.W. & Paull, S. (1995). A comprehensive approach to family focused services. In L. Morrow (Ed.), *Family literacy: Connections in schools and communities*, 167-83. Newark, DE: International Reading Association.

Powell, D.R. (1995). Teaching parenting and basic skills to parents: What we know. A paper presented at Research Design Symposium on Family Literacy, U.S. Department. of Education, Office of Educational Research and Improvement, Washington, DC, Sept. 7-8, 1995.

Purcell-Gates, V. (1994). *The relationships between parental literacy skills and functional uses of print and children's ability to learn literacy skills.* Cambridge, MA: Harvard University Graduate School of Education.

Snow, C.E. & Goldfield, B.A. (1983). Turn the page please: Situation-specific language acquisition. *Journal of Child Language*, 10, 535-49.

Snow, C.E., Barnes, W.S., Chandler, J., Goodman, I.F. & Hemphill, L. (1991). *Unfulfilled expectations: Home and school influences on literacy.* Cambridge, MA: Harvard University Press.

Taylor, D. & Dorsey-Gaines, C. (1988). *Growing up literate: Learning from inner-city families.* Portsmouth, NH: Heinemann.

Teale, W.H. & Sulzby, E. (1986). Home background and young children's literacy development. In *Emergent literacy: Writing and reading*, 173-206. Norwood, NJ: ABLEX.

Topping, K. J. (1986) *Parents as educators.* London: Croom Helm.

Tracey, D.H. & Young, J.W. (1994). Mother-child interactions during children's oral reading at home. In D. Leu & C. Kinzer (Eds.), *Multidimensional aspects of literacy research, theory, and practice.* (Forty-third Yearbook of the National Reading Conference, 342-50. Chicago, IL: National Reading Conference.

Tracey, D.H. (1995). Children practicing reading at home: What we know about how parents help. In L. Morrow (Ed.), *Family literacy: Connections in schools and communities*, 253-68. Newark, DE: International Reading Association.

Teaching Parenting and Basic Skills to Parents: What We Know

Douglas Powell
Purdue University

The history of programmatic efforts to influence parents' knowledge and skills regarding child rearing has a long and rich history. However, many important questions remain unanswered. Fortunately, in the past three decades there has been an important increase in the quality and quantity of studies focused on program outcomes and on parenting. While not robust, existing research collectively points directly or indirectly to the importance of five characteristics or elements of programs designed to support or change parents' behaviors. The five areas are addressed below, and lessons learned in each of the five areas are described.

New Knowledge Interacts with Existing Beliefs and Practices

Research points to the value of *guided opportunities to incorporate new information and skills into existing beliefs and skills related to parenting and interactions with children.*

> *In a review of outcome studies of 20 early intervention programs targeted at some aspect of family functioning, analysts concluded that more pervasive and sustained effects are likely to be realized when the intervention includes 11 or more contacts over at least a three-month period. Researchers suggest that a certain duration of contact is essential to the development of a trusting relationship between family and program.*

Parenting is an active, cognitive process. Accordingly, program designs that enable parents to digest and integrate new perspectives on parenting with existing beliefs and practices are likely to yield greater effects than program designs that approach parents primarily as "blank slates" to be written upon with all new knowledge.

Beliefs are cognitive representations of reality (Sigel, 1985) that shape parents' socialization and teaching actions. Parents have been found to hold simultaneously a number of different beliefs regarding how their children learn and become socialized, with approximately 87 percent of all stated beliefs falling into one of the following four categories:

- cognitive processes (child learns through thinking and reasoning, considering options, drawing in references, weighing consequences);

- direct instruction (child learns from being told what to do, from explanations or advice);

- positive feedback (child learns through experiencing success, approval, and support); and

- negative feedback (child learns through being punished or criticized for behavior) (Sigel, Stinson & Flaughter, 1991).

Pertinent to family literacy programs are the beliefs held by parents regarding the requisites of their child's early success in school. A study using a national sample found that parents and kindergarten teachers had similar views on the importance of some characteristics for kindergarten (e.g., child is curious, enthusiastic

---

about learning), but had dissimilar beliefs about the importance of other characteristics (e.g., the ability to count to 20, to know the alphabet). For example, most parents (59 percent), but few kindergarten teachers (7 percent), indicated it is very important or essential for a child to be able to count to 20 (West, Hausken & Collins, 1993). (For a review of the literature on school readiness, see Powell, 1995.)

Core beliefs about parenting and children's development may reflect deeply held values and stem from influential origins; some ideas are like cherished possessions, modified or abandoned reluctantly (Abelson, 1986). Multiple factors influence the development and maintenance of parents' beliefs. Among these factors, those outside the home include: cultural values and traditions; socio-economic status; work; social networks of relatives, friends, and neighbors; and advice from experts. Factors within the home include the characteristics of parents, themselves, (e.g., developmental history, psychological attributes, age, gender); marital relationship; and characteristics of the child (Okagaki & Divecha, 1994).

Of course, individuals often are slow to change their ideas even in the face of compelling information, and may disregard or distort new information or use it selectively, if new ideas conflict with perceived vested interests (Goodnow & Collins, 1990). For instance, a recent qualitative, longitudinal study of low-income, single mothers found that mothers were receptive to information from "experts" when these perspectives furthered their goals for their children; their ideas about preschool learning were linked to culturally driven models of child rearing, including respect for authority and contributing to one's family or community (Holloway, Rambaud, Fuller & Eggers-Pierola, in press).

Discussion is viewed widely as a promising strategy for parents to think about new information in relation to existing perspectives on parenting. The adult education literature long has suggested that personal experience be used as a learning resource, and that programs include a strong experiential component (e.g., Brookfield, 1986). Discussion is an opportunity for parents to digest new information and insight within existing belief frameworks.

While more needs to be known about the conditions under which parents modify their beliefs and practices, research suggests that long-term parent discussion groups can be a powerful tool in facilitating change in the values and teaching styles of low-income mothers (Slaughter, 1983), and the child-rearing beliefs and practices of middle-class mothers and fathers (Powell, 1994). Dialogue was the primary intervention tool in a program aimed at helping socially and geographically isolated, low-income mothers "gain a voice" and become more actively engaged in conceptualizing and interacting with their children in ways that would promote cognitive development and a sense of self-competence. In fact, an evaluation found the program increased participants' perceived social support and the complexity of their understandings of knowledge and its development (Bond, Belenky & Weinstock, 1992).

In one longitudinal study, informal discussions among parents during a program's break (what the investigators called "kitchen talk," because the break occurred in a kitchen) were found to be as novel or nonroutine as discussions guided by staff during the formal segment of the program (Powell & Eisenstadt, 1988). Thus, an informal exchange of ideas among peers may offer perspectives that extend and perhaps even challenge existing knowledge, beliefs, and practices.

Today, disregard for parents' existing beliefs and practices by parent education programs has generated considerable criticism and ethical concern. All interventions impose an idea of "the good, the desirable, and the healthy" (Sigel, 1983, p. 8), and a dominant professional role in parent education programs may undermine parents' sense of confidence (Hess, 1980). For programs aimed at ethnic and language minority populations, the imposition of the dominant culture's standards of parenting may be viewed as an attempt to "melt away sociocultural diversity" (Laosa, 1983, p. 337).

Several safeguards have been recommended to prevent manipulations of a parent's goals and excessive pressure to alter existing beliefs and behaviors, including clarity in communications about a program's theoretical orientation, and respect for a parent's child-rearing values (Brim, 1959; Sigel, 1983), along with a collaborative role for the professional involved (Cochran & Woolever, 1982; Hess, 1980). Thus, the respectful, non-intrusive professional role recommended in the literature on the ethics of parent education programs coincides with images of an appropriate professional role derived from the literature on parents' beliefs and change processes described earlier.

Parenting in Context

The teaching of parenting skills to parents should *actively acknowledge the relation of parenting beliefs and behaviors to other aspects of individual functioning, including social skills and job-related experiences.* Parenting issues cannot be readily compartmentalized and adequately addressed in isolation. Family literacy programs provide many opportunities to build on inextricable connections among parenting and other adult roles and skills. Particularly promising are options to integrate and to use similar or complementary pedagogical strategies in the adult and parent education components of any program.

Research findings underscore the central role of parenting in intricate patterns of beliefs and behaviors. From studies of intervention programs, one lesson teaches that efforts to address parenting cannot be meaningfully separated from the parent's interpersonal relationship skills. For example, an intervention program at the University of Washington attempted to implement a two-step approach to working with "high-risk" mothers, beginning with social skills training and then moving on to child-rearing knowledge and behavior. It was assumed that a mother's interpersonal competence was a necessary condition for improving a mother's child-rearing abilities. However, program workers (mental health nurses) discovered it was impossible to avoid parent-child relationship issues in the social skills component of the intervention, as parenting

issues surfaced repeatedly in the social skills training (Booth, Mitchell, Barnard & Spieker, 1989).

From studies of work and family life, one learns that work exposes an individual to experiences and ideas that influence parenting styles and beliefs. A study of the effects of participatory work strategies in a manufacturing plant on the employee's family roles found that employees involved in decision-making and problem-solving at all levels of the work setting, primarily through small work teams, reported using the "team meeting" concept at home and using communication skills that had been learned during work training sessions. Illustrative of the findings, one father reported that his participatory experiences on the job had led him to ". . . use some of the things we do at work" with his son, "instead of yelling" at the boy (Crouter, 1984). Other research has found a connection between conditions of the work setting (autonomy vs. compliance) and parenting values and practices (with emphasis on self-initiative vs. conformity) (Kohn, 1969; Luster, Rhoades & Haas, 1989).

The parenting-in-context theme also includes the idea that efforts to influence parent beliefs and practices should *tailor the introduction of new information and skills to family realities and to the quality of the parent-child relationship.* Several areas of research and cumulative program experience point to the merits of "beginning where parents are."

An early, indirect indicator of the need to acknowledge the ecology of parenthood in parenting programs appeared in the 1960s and early 1970s, when numerous parent education methods frequently used with middle-class populations were applied unsuccessfully to lower-income parents. A reviewer of these failed initiatives concluded that environmental *reality factors* such as marital disruption, financial instability, and inadequate housing worked against effective use of group methods with low-income parents, ". . . unless the group was supplemented by other services" (Chilman, 1973).

The instructional strategy of helping students *conditionalize* their knowledge by pursuing an everyday problem-oriented versus fact- or discipline-oriented introduction of information—posited as an effective way to support the transfer of information or skills to a variety of settings (Bransford, Goldman & Vye, 1991)—has special significance in teaching skills related to parenting. Specifically, the individuality of a child often is used by parents to disregard the global advice or recommendations of experts. In fact, it is possible to agree with an expert's idea but at the same time reject that idea by claiming simply ". . . it's a good idea, but it just wouldn't work with my child" (Goodnow & Collins, 1990, p. 102). Accordingly, parents who acquire knowledge and skills that are tailored to characteristics or issues regarding a particular child are likely to use the new information because it is pertinent to their individual situation. Conversely, when experts offer vague advice, it is less likely that parents will derive sophisticated ideas or practices from such advice (Sameroff & Feil, 1985).

Research on the benefits of joint parent-child book reading also underscores the importance of considering context (i.e., parent-child relationship) in which prescriptions for parenting are to be applied. There is strong evidence that parent-child reading is related to a number of child successes in learning to read (Bus, van IJzendoorn & Pellegrini, 1995). While these findings lend support to the wisdom of attempts to encourage joint parent-child book reading in family literacy programs, they need to be qualified in a manner that considers the "condition" of the parent-child relationship. Studies show that in parent-child *dyads*, where there is an insecure attachment, the parent is less sensitive to the needs and cues of the child and the joys of reading a book probably are minimal or nonexistent; in fact, such a situation may have a negative effect on the child's emergent literacy skills and interests (Bus & van IJzendoorn, 1988).

The principle of "beginning where parents are" is consistent with the social-contextual model of family literacy that asks, "How can we draw on parents' knowledge and experience to inform instruction?" rather than, "How can we transfer school practices into home contexts?" (Auerbach, 1989, p. 177). (This model is built upon the

conditions and concerns of specific communities, and does not involve a predetermined curriculum.)

Maintaining Balance

If a mother isn't making it financially, and she's just had a fight with her boyfriend, and he's just split, there ain't no way I can say to her, "OK, let's you and I go play a game with the child," (Mindick, 1986, p. 83).

The above words of a home visitor capture the problem of maintaining focus on the child and on parenting issues when the content boundaries of a parenting program are broadened to include sensitivity to, or intentional efforts to address, adult issues and family functioning. Multiple-focus programs assume that pressing factors in the environment or within the parent often interfere with the parent's ability to attend to the child and to the information and suggestions of the home visitor. Unmet basic needs (such as shelter and health care) may be viewed, for example, as a cause of parents' giving low priority to professionally prescribed regimens for handicapped children (Dunst & Trivette, 1988).

Evaluations of multiple-focused programs point to a tendency for child development matters to be ignored or overshadowed by "major issues" facing the parent or family (e.g., Mindick, 1986). However, limited attention to child development content in multiple-focus home visiting programs may have a limited (or no) effect upon the child.

The evaluation results of the Child and Family Resource Program (CFRP) may be interpreted as suggesting that family circumstances, but not child outcomes, were improved by the program, as the content of home visits focused almost exclusively on family needs (Travers, Nauta & Irwin, 1982). Hence, an important lesson is that programs should *maintain a balanced, concrete focus on parenting and child development content.*

The CFRP evaluation findings raise questions about program designs based upon the assumption that a primary focus on improving family circumstances will lead to improved child outcomes. It appears that changes in child outcomes require concentrated attention to parenting and child issues, but not at the expense of ignoring pressing family circumstances. Thus, the theme of organizing program content around family realities needs to be qualified to emphasize the necessity of a clear agenda regarding parenting and child issues. Certainly, the program's role of helping parents maintain a "child's eye view" of events, situations, and relationships appears central to achieving improved outcomes for children.

Intensity Matters

The above descriptions of the origins and malleability of parents' ideas and practices, coupled with program experiences pointing to the value as well as pitfalls of attending to family circumstances, set the stage for the lesson that parenting skills cannot be taught "on the cheap." Research points to the importance of *providing long-term, intensive work with parents, especially those living in high-risk circumstances.*

Quite simply, the magnitude of program effects increases, if programs are intensive. Brief encounters between a program and a parent will not dramatically alter or strengthen the pattern of parenting or improve child outcomes.

In a review of outcome studies of 20 early intervention programs targeted at some aspect of family functioning, analysts concluded that more pervasive and sustained effects are likely to be realized when the intervention includes 11 or more contacts over at least a three-month period. Researchers suggest that a certain duration of contact is essential to the development of a trusting relationship between family and program. The 20 programs included in this review were initiated at some time in the period from pregnancy to the first three months of the baby's life, and included populations representing a range of socio-economic status (Heinecke, Beckwith & Thompson, 1988).

Recent evaluation results from the Even Start Family Literacy Program indicate that the amount of time parents participated in parenting education through Even Start was positively related to their

child's receptive vocabulary (St. Pierre, Swartz, Gamse, Murray, Deck & Nickel, 1995).

Concluding Comment

The lessons reviewed herein provide points of departure for designing programs that are likely to yield a significant, positive impact upon parenting. At the same time, key questions remain unanswered. The amount of structure that is appropriate for program workers, for example, is unclear; and thoughtful program development efforts are needed to demonstrate workable strategies for maintaining a balanced, responsive program focus on child and family issues.

Family literacy programs are a field-based "laboratory" for generating research and program development initiatives that may advance the field's understanding of how best to support adults in their child-rearing roles. The focused attention on literacy within an intergenerational family framework is an ideal setting for implementing, refining, and extending the lessons described in this paper, and for enabling all in the field to learn new and valuable lessons.

References

Abelson, R.P. (1986). Beliefs are like possessions. *Journal for the Theory of Social Behavior, 16,* 223-50.

Auerbach, E.R. (1989). Toward a social-contextual approach to family literacy. *Harvard Educational Review, 59,* 165-81.

Bond, L.A., Belenky, M.F. & Weinstock, J.S. (1992). Listening partners: Helping rural mothers find a voice. *Family Resource Coalition Report, 11,* 18-19.

Booth, C.L., Mitchell, S.L., Barnard, K.E. & Spieker, S.J. (1989). Development of maternal skills in multiproblem families: Effects on the mother-child relationship. *Developmental Psychology, 25,* 403-12.

Bransford, J.D., Goldman, S.R. & Vye, N.J. (1991). Making a difference in people's abilities to think: Reflections on a decade of work and some hopes for the future. In L. Okagaki & R.L. Sternberg (Eds.), *Directors of development: Influences on the development of children's thinking*, 147-80. Hillsdale, NJ: Lawrence Erlbaum.

Brim, O.G. (1959). *Education for child rearing.* New York: Russell Sage Foundation.

Brookfield, S. (1986). *Understanding and facilitating adult learning.* San Francisco, CA: Jossey Bass.

Bus, A.G. & van IJzendoorn, M.H. (1988). Mother-child interactions, attachment and emergent literacy: A cross-sectional study. *Child Development, 59,* 1262-72.

Bus, A.G., van IJzendoorn, M.H. & Pellegrini, A.D. (1995). Joint book reading makes for success in learning to read: A meta-analysis on intergenerational transmission of literacy. *Review of Educational Research, 65,* 1-21.

Chilman, C.S. (1973). Programs for disadvantaged parents. In B.M. Caldwell & H.N. Ricciuti (Eds.), *Review of Child Development Research. 3,* 403-65. Chicago: University of Chicago Press.

Cochran, M. & Woolever, F. (1983). Beyond the deficit model: The empowerment of parents with information and informal supports. In I. E. Sigel & L. M. Laosa (Eds), *Changing families,* 225-45. New York: Plenum.

Crouter, A.C. (1984). Participative work as an influence on human development. *Human Development, 5,* 71-90.

Dunst, C.J. & Trivette, C.M. (1988). A family systems model of early intervention with handicapped and developmentally at-risk children. In D.R. Powell (Ed.), *Parent education as early childhood intervention,* 31-179. Norwood, NJ: Ablex.

Goodnow, J.J. & Collins, W.A. (1990). *Development according to parents: The nature, sources, and consequences of parents' ideas.* Hillsdale, NJ: Lawrence Erlbaum.

Heinecke, C.M., Beckwith, L. & Thompson, A (1988). Early intervention in the family system: A framework and review. *Infant Mental Health Journal, 9,* 111-41.

Hess, R.D. (1980). Experts and amateurs: Some unintended consequences of parent education. In M.D. Fantini & R. Cardenes (Eds.), *Parenting in a multicultural society,* 141-59. New York: Longman.

Holloway, S.D., Rambaud, M.F., Fuller, B. & Eggers-Pierola, C. (in press). What is "appropriate practice" at home and in child care? Low-income mothers' views on preparing their children for school. *Early Childhood Research Quarterly.*

Kohn, M.L. (1969). *Class and conformity: A study in values.* Homewood, IL: The Dorsey Press.

Laosa, L.M. (1983). Parent education, cultural pluralism, and public policy: The uncertain connection. In R. Haskins & D. Adams (Eds.), *Parent education and public policy,* 331-45. Norwood, NJ: Ablex.

Luster, R., Rhoades, K. & Haas, B. (1989). The relation between parental values and parenting behavior: A test of the Kohn hypothesis. *Journal of Marriage and the Family, 51,* 139-47.

Mindick, B. (1986). *Social engineering in family matters.* New York: Praeger.

Okagaki, L. & Divecha, D.J. (1993). Development of parental beliefs. In T. Luster & L. Okagaki (Eds.), *Parenting: An Ecological Perspective,* 35-67. Hillsdale, NJ: Lawrence Erlbaum.

Powell, D.R. (1994). Effects of information and social support during the early years of parenthood: A longitudinal study of MELD. Final technical report to the Bush Foundation. West Lafayette, IN: Purdue University.

Powell, D.R. (1995). Enabling young children to succeed in school. Washington, DC: American Educational Research Association

Powell, D.R. & Eisenstadt, J.W. (1988). Informal and formal conversations in parent education groups: An observational study. *Family Relations, 37,* 166-70.

Sameroff, A.J. & Feil, L.A. (1985). Parental concepts of development. In I.E. Sigel (Ed.), *Parental belief systems: The psychological consequences for children,* 83-105. Hillsdale, NJ: Lawrence Erlbaum.

Sigel, I.E. (1985). A conceptual analysis of beliefs. In I.E. Sigel (Ed.), *Parental belief systems: The psychological consequences for children,* 347-71. Hillsdale, NJ: Lawrence Erlbaum.

Sigel, I.E., Stinson, E.T. & Flaugher, J. (1991). Socialization of representational competence in the family: The distancing paradigm. In L. Okagaki & R.J. Sternberg (Eds.), *Directors of development: Influences on the development of children's thinking*, 121-44. Hillsdale, NJ: Lawrence Erlbaum.

Slaughter, D.R. (1983). Early intervention and its effects on maternal and child development. Monographs of the Society for Research in Child Development, 48 (4), (Serial No. 202).

St. Pierre, R., Swartz, J., Gamse, B., Murray, S., Deck, D. & Nickel, P. (1995). National evaluation of the Even Start family literacy program. Final report to the Office of the Under Secretary, U.S. Department of Education. Cambridge, MA: Abt Associates, Inc.

Travers, J., Nauta, M. & Irwin, N. (1982). The effects of a social program: Final report of the Child and Family Resource Program's infant-toddler component. Cambridge, MA: Abt Associates.

West, J., Hausken, E.G. & Collins, M. (1993). Readiness for kindergarten: Parent and teacher beliefs. Washington, DC: National Center for Education Statistics, Office of Educational Research and Improvement, U.S. Department of Education (NCES 93-257).

Intergenerational Transfer of Literacy

Catherine Snow and Patton Tabors
Harvard Graduate School of Education

This paper provides an analysis of findings related to the intergenerational transfer of literacy, in particular familial attitudes, behavior, and characteristics that seem to promote literacy achievement in children. The issue motivating this analysis is a search for mechanisms that explain why children from some families arrive at school better prepared for literacy achievement than others—and how some families continue to support their children's literacy achievement, after they are in school. It is clear that, in general, more literate and highly educated parents have children who perform better in school. Our problem is not so much the difficulty of seeking a reason for this fact, but rather the challenge of selecting from among a multitude of possible explanations. We take as our task in this paper, therefore, to assess the many, disparate explanations of parental effects on children's literacy in an attempt to understand the most powerful influences, and to recommend how such mechanisms for learning might be integrated into potentially successful family literacy programs.

> *Vocabulary has been associated with literacy development across a variety of studies . . . . Parenting classes within family literacy programs could well focus on . . . community, church and school-related activities as a source of varied conversational topics, during which new vocabulary and more complex ideas might well be introduced into the home.*

Social Class Differences

A starting point for much of the previous work on familial influences on literacy has been the evidence associated with social class differences in reading achievement. Thirty years ago, public attention was alerted to evidence that socio-economic status was related to differences in school achievement (Coleman et al., 1966). *Equality of Educational Opportunity* revealed that the educational deficit of children from low-income families was present at school entry and increased with each year they stayed in school. These findings of social class differences in school achievement have been confirmed dozens of times since, in comparisons within and across school systems and in every National Assessment of Educational Progress (NAEP) report. The 1981 report from the NAEP, for example, indicated that the reading achievement of children in affluent suburban schools was significantly and consistently higher than that of children in "disadvantaged" urban schools, and the 1985 NAEP report on reading found that low-income 17-year-olds could read only on an elementary school level (a level achieved by advantaged students at age 13). Not surprisingly, conventional wisdom has held that any factor present in middle-class homes is likely to be positive for school learning, whereas factors present in working-class homes work against achievement.

In fact, though, it is difficult to isolate the factors that may produce a given effect simply by comparing middle-class to working-class children. Social class is a "package variable"—a summary label for an intricate complex of related variables including parental education, occupational status, income, housing conditions, time allocation, attitudes toward school and schooling, experiences with school, expectations for future educational and occupational success, nature of the family's social network, style of parent-child interaction, and many more elements. Replicating findings of social class differences in school achievement brings us no closer to understanding the mechanisms by which those differences develop because it is rarely possible to sort out the separate effects of the wide array of factors packaged together as "working class" or "middle class."

Complexity of Literacy

A further difficulty in sorting out the mechanisms that explain familial effects on child literacy is the nature of literacy itself. Literacy is not a single skill that simply gets better with age or instruction. We contend that being literate means different things to the skilled first-grader, or fourth-grader, or high school student or adult. Just as the effects of school experiences can be quite different at different points in a child's development (see, for example, Alexander & Entwistle, 1988), so also can the effects of certain familial practices related to literacy development.

The actual problem is to decide *when* we would like to assess or characterize the familial effects on child literacy. Much of the research in this area has focused on early effects, to explain differences observable in children on school entry. Social class differences, however, increase in magnitude as children continue in school—suggesting that familial effects account for more than just differences in emergent literacy skill. A discussion of the mechanisms of family effects, then, must distinguish familial influences in terms of what aspect of literacy they influence as well as how that influence is exerted.

Mechanisms of Intergenerational Transfer

During the last 25 years, a variety of mechanisms have been proposed to improve familial effects on child literacy. In this section of the paper, we will review research supporting each of these candidate mechanisms, prior to assessing them as possible explanations for family effects on children's acquisition of literacy.

Simple Transfer

Much research in the field of literacy development documents straightforward transfer effects (i.e., parental literacy skills and behaviors are transmitted directly to children through activities like picture book reading and writing shopping lists). It is worth noting, however, that most of these effects have been documented during the preschool and kindergarten period (i.e., effects on emergent literacy skills rather than on sophisticated reading). Dyadic book-reading, for example, has been identified as a source of knowledge about print (Clay, 1979), letters (Burgess, 1982), and the characteristics of written registers (Feitelson, Bracha & Goldstein, 1986; Purcell-Gates, 1988). Belief in the efficacy of book-reading as a site for direct transfer of print-related knowledge has been a source of intervention programs (e.g., 'little books' sent home to Spanish-speaking families in California (Goldenberg, Reese & Gallimore, 1992), and Feitelson's classroom library movement (Shimron, 1994) in Israel). The presence of refrigerator letters, posters, paper for making lists, newspapers, and books in the home, and parental efforts to direct children's attention to environmental print have similarly been assumed to promote child literacy, through a direct transfer mechanism (Toomey & Sloan, 1994; Goodman, 1984; Harste, Woodward & Burke, 1984).

Transfer explanations account nicely for social class differences, particularly in the skills of kindergarten children. Social class differences in child performance do not disappear with the supplementation of parental transfer of print knowledge through interventions like Sesame Street and Head Start. Nowadays, most children, even those from families where the parents have little or no education, arrive at kindergarten able to sing the alphabet song and to recognize letters—but the long-term literacy achievement of children from poor families has not improved.

A major criticism of the simple transfer view is that literacy consists of much more than the print skills that can be transferred during book-reading, attention to ambient print, or collaborations on early writing tasks. Furthermore, many children who will go on to be successful readers have, in fact, not learned anything about letters or their shapes, names, or sounds, during their preschool years. In Scandinavia, for example, where adult literacy rates are the highest in the world, parents are discouraged from teaching their children anything about print before they enter school at age 7, suggesting that the powerful effects of collaboration go far beyond the transfer of specific bits and pieces of literacy knowledge.

Participation in Literacy Practice

One alternative view of parental effects defines literacy as social practice, thus emphasizing the parental role in generating a set of literate practices in which children can participate. Literacy is seen as a natural reaction to certain societal needs, an easy reinvention by children in order to solve problems they encounter (Goodman, 1986). According to this view, one major parental role, then, is to model literacy as a practice useful in solving problems, and to establish social literacy practices that children can participate in as a critical part of their lives, rather than simply transmitting or transferring literacy.

Those who emphasize literacy as social practice tend also to believe that literacy is relatively ubiquitous and argue that even very uneducated families engage regularly in the use of literacy (Leichter, 1974; Taylor & Dorsey-Gaines, 1988), though the specific purposes for which literacy is used may differ from family to family. If literacy is, indeed, a cultural practice more than a psycholinguistic skill, then children for whom the purposes and rules of school literacy are unfamiliar and obscure might well be expected to fail through unfamiliarity. It could be argued, though, that the various uses of literacy differ in level as well as in type—that families who use literacy only to make lists, recite from the Bible, or fill in forms are displaying lower-level, as well as socially and culturally distinct, literacy skills.

Some have criticized the social practice theorists by pointing out that there are many families, even in the United States, in which literacy practices are essentially absent, and the ubiquitous print of the larger environment is invisible to family members. Purcell-Gates (1995), for example, studied an urban Appalachian family in which both parents were illitrate, and practices such as using street signs to find directions, using food labels in shopping, or noting the arrival of mail were totally unfamiliar. Needless to say, the children in this family encountered enormous problems at school, among which their ignorance of the possible uses of literacy was as great as their unfamiliarity with letters and written words.

The social practice view of literacy tends to go hand-in-hand with a view of literacy as relatively easily acquired and more or less universal—a view in which the mechanism of parental effect is clearly specified, but in which it is very hard to extract an explanation for the fact that some children raised in literate homes fail to become good readers. Indeed, the only possible explanation for failure in the acquisition of literacy at school is that the literacy practices a child knows from home are not valued at school (i.e., that there is a home-school mismatch).

Enjoyment and Engagement

Noting enormous individual differences in skills of children from similarly literate backgrounds (differences even among children from the same family), other researchers have sought mechanisms of parental effects that can explain variation in outcomes. One group emphasizes the value of establishing positive affect around literacy activities as a route to the child's development of active engagement in literacy tasks. Those who hold this view would argue, for example, that the positive effects of dyadic book-reading on child literacy derive primarily from the enjoyment that is associated with books and the linking of literacy with one-on-one parental attention and affection. Successful parental intervention programs emphasize making book-reading fun and enjoyable (e.g., selecting books of interest to the child and responding to child interests) (Svensson, 1995). Children, it is assumed, learn from their parents that literacy is a source of enjoyment, and the enjoyment they experience motivates them to persist through the often difficult early stages of literacy acquisition.

Views regarding the importance of affect in helping to explain literacy outcomes are supported by the demonstrated increase in the complexity of the reading matter one can comprehend, if the topic is of interest (Scollon & Scollon, 1981). Furthermore, reading with engagement and expectation of enjoyment leads to more time spent reading, i.e., more practice, and thus greater fluency—a major predictor of long-term reading outcomes.

Of course, as Csikszentmihalyi (1991) points out, many children have sufficient extrinsic motivation to keep them involved in literacy acquisition, since they believe parents' and teachers' precepts that literacy is a prerequisite to school success and achievement in later life. But for children who have less reason to believe in literacy as a route to success (e.g., minority children with adult acquaintances who are unemployed even when well educated), entry into a state of high level enjoyment while reading—'the flow' to use Csikszentmihalyi's term—may be crucial to keeping children focused on literacy long enough to make serious gains.

Linguistic and Cognitive Mechanisms

Finally, other researchers have argued that the parental role is most crucial in helping children to develop oral linguistic precursors to literacy, such as a sophisticated vocabulary and extended discourse skills, rather than literacy skills, themselves, which can be easily acquired at school, if language prerequisites are in place.

Vocabulary has been associated with literacy development across a variety of studies for children speaking different languages and learning to read in a variety of instructional settings (Anderson & Freebody, 1981). One of the ways that a larger vocabulary might promote reading is obvious in a language like English, where the pronunciation of words is not easily predictable from their spelling. In this case, knowing what the word might be can help eliminate mispronunciations and misidentifications in most cases. However, vocabulary also predicts literacy in languages like Spanish, in which the spelled

form is absolutely unambiguous as to pronunciation. It seems likely, then, that vocabulary knowledge in these cases indexes world knowledge—background information that the reader can use to help in the task of comprehension.

One might expect that children in families who talk a lot have larger vocabularies. In fact, talking a lot might not correlate with talking in ways that introduce relatively sophisticated lexical items. In our work studying 75 low-income families with preschool aged children—the Home-School Study of Language and Literacy Development (HSSLD)—we have found that families who use more sophisticated or rarer vocabulary, i.e., vocabulary that goes beyond the 8,500 most common words in the English language, are the families whose children score well on the Peabody Picture Vocabulary Test, a test of receptive vocabulary given when the children are five years old (Beals & Tabors, 1995). It seems, then, that exposure to less common, more sophisticated vocabulary at home relates directly to children's vocabulary acquisition.

Beyond vocabulary, though, performance on tasks like describing pictures or telling stories in a way that is relatively complete, detailed, and comprehensible relates to reading. Telling stories and describing pictures have in common the demand to produce extended discourse. Extended discourse emerges when talk deals with complicated events or topics, when a simple story is embellished by making connections to feelings, related events, causes and implications, when talk moves beyond facts to explanation, or beyond opinion to argumentation.

One might expect that children learn how to do this sort of thing from participating in opportunities at home to hear or provide extended texts—e.g., opportunities at dinner to tell about their day or to listen to their parents explain something complicated. In fact, results from the Home-School Study confirm that this is the case (Beals, De Temple, & Dickinson, 1994; Snow & Kurland, in press). It seems, then, that opportunities to engage in extended discourse in the home build skills in producing extended discourse of precisely the type that is needed for high levels of literacy.

Implications for Family Literacy Programs

While family literacy programs are generally aware of the importance of teaching the basic skills related to literacy and often promote book reading as a joint literacy activity between parents and children, these programs may not include activities which would promote literacy as social practice or focus on the need for rich oral language interactions, both of which are necessary to support children's development of the full range of literacy skills. Representative suggestions for how these aspects of literacy could be introduced into the four components of family literacy programs—adult education classes, early childhood education classes, parenting classes, and parent-child interaction periods (Darling, 1995)—follow.

Adult education classes, whether in the form of adult literacy or General Educational Development (GED) preparation classes, could make a greater contribution to family literacy if one of their goals was to develop their students' self-images as "readers" and "writers." By developing these sorts of self-images, these programs can convey a sense of both the functional and entertainment value of reading and writing. Parents with positive attitudes towards literacy will buy books for themselves and their children, will model reading and writing behaviors, and will create home environments in which literacy practices are common and viewed as engaging.

Early childhood education classrooms within family literacy programs are ideal settings for the introduction of rich oral language opportunities. Researchers have found that staff members who sit down at snack times and mealtimes with children in early childhood classrooms, for example, raise the level of conversation by maintaining topic continuity and introducing complex syntax and vocabulary (Dickinson, Cote, & Smith, 1994). Dress-up corners create a context for small groups of children to engage in fantasy play, which has been found to involve much more extended

discourse than whole class activities or seat work. Engaging children in active, analytic talk during book reading generates gains not seen if books are simply read to children, without questions and opportunities for discussion. In general, small group activities generate more participation and active talk from children than activities in larger groups, and the systematic introduction of novel, challenging content (e.g., a science corner, books about faraway places, discussions of field trips) creates a context in which sophisticated vocabulary and world knowledge can be developed. Family literacy programs which include quality early childhood education components can capitalize on all of these opportunities for exposing children to rich oral language.

We know too little about the mechanisms for supporting richer parent-child talk during interactions. Although Whitehurst (1988) has successfully trained both parents and preschool teachers in a technique which he calls "dialogic reading," which has been shown to produce gains in children's language, there has been no research on how to stimulate more sophisticated adult talk in general contexts, e.g., during mealtimes or while riding the bus. Family literacy programs which incorporate parent-child interaction periods might well be an ideal setting for research on the development and application of techniques for encouraging this type of talk between parents and children. Such work is necessary if family literacy programs are to do the best job possible of promoting parent-child conversation during interactions.

Interesting conversations are not likely to occur in the absence of interesting topics. Research by Snow and her colleagues (1991) and by Anderson, Wilson, and Fielding (1988) demonstrates that parents who are engaged in a wider variety of activities (e.g., political action, social engagements, work outside the home, etc.) have children who are better readers. This relationship is presumably mediated by the more interesting conversations such parents can engage in with their children. Parenting classes within family literacy programs could well focus on the value of parental participation in community, church and school-related activities as a source of varied conversational topics, during which new vocabulary and more complex ideas might well be introduced into the home.

Conclusion

We have seen evidence that families support literacy development via direct transfer of knowledge about print, by engaging their children in literate practices, by ensuring that literacy activities are both fun and meaningful, by modelling the uses of literacy in the home, and by providing opportunities for children to develop the language skills that will be prerequisite to higher level literacy functioning. Clearly, all these mechanisms might well be at work. Precisely because literacy is a complex capacity that changes as children grow, and that has prerequisites in several different domains of knowledge, the sources of familial support for literacy development are likely to be multiple and varied.

The most widely cited familial supports (transfer of knowledge about print and participation in the culture of literacy) may be of particular importance for children just entering literacy—these are the familial behaviors that distinguish successful versus unsuccessful kindergarteners and first-graders. Family-induced motivation to pursue literacy and family-generated language abilities, on the other hand, may exert their influence throughout the elementary school years. Reading tasks change character most notably in the middle of elementary school, when children are first expected to read complex, sophisticated texts and to learn new material through reading; at this point, the motivation to persist and oral familiarity with the types of language used in text may be crucial prerequisites to success.

In the process of seeking the mechanisms for social support of literacy development, researchers have, in effect, redefined literacy, itself, as a far more complex process than was conceived in the past. Furthermore, the views of the ways in which the family might play a role in literacy development also have been expanded and diversified. The challenge facing us as we work to improve family literacy programs, then, is to analyze the family's role so as to understand how to help families provide a full range of aids to their children's literacy development.

References

Alexander, K. & Entwistle, D. (1988). Achievement in the first two years of school: Patterns and processes. *Monographs of the Society for Research in Child Development*, 218, 53(2).

Anderson, R. & Freebody, P. (1981). Vocabulary knowledge. In J.T. Guthrie (Ed.), *Comprehension and teaching: Research reviews*, 77-117. Newark, DE: International Reading Association.

Anderson, R., Wilson, P. & Fielding, L. (1988). Growth in reading and how children spend their time outside of school. *Reading Research Quarterly*, 23, 285-303.

Beals, D. & Tabors, P. (1995). Arboretum, bureaucratic, and carbohydrates: Preschoolers' exposure to rare vocabulary at home. *First Language*, 5, 57-76.

Beals, D., De Temple, J. & Dickinson, D. (1994). Talking and listening that support early literacy development of children from low-income families. In D. Dickinson (Ed.), *Bridges to literacy: Children, families, and schools*, 19-42. Cambridge, MA: Blackwell.

Burgess, J. (1982). The effects of a training program for parents of preschoolers on the children's school readiness. *Reading Improvement*, 19, 313-18.

Clay, M. (1979). *Reading: The patterning of complex behavior*. Portsmouth, NH: Heinemann.

Coleman, J., Campbell, E., Hobson, C., McPartland, J., Mood, A., Weinfeld, F. & York, R. (1966). *Equality of educational opportunity*. Washington, DC: U.S. Office of Education, National Center for Educational Statistics.

Csikszentmihalyi, M. (1991). Literacy and intrinsic motivation. In S. Graubard (Ed.), *Literacy: An Overview By Fourteen Experts*, 115-40. New York: The Noonday Press.

Darling, S. (1995). Personal communication, Washington, DC, September 8.

Dickinson, D., Cote, L. & Smith, M. (1994). Learning vocabulary in preschool: Social and discourse contexts affecting vocabulary growth. In C. Daiute (Ed.), *The development of literacy through social interaction.* San Francisco: Jossey-Bass.

Feitelson, D., Bracha, K. & Goldstein, Z. (1986). Effects of listening series stories on first graders' comprehension and use of language. *Research in the Training of English, 20,* 339-50.

Goldenberg, C. Reese, L., & Gallimore, R. (1992). Effects of literacy materials from school on Latino children's home experiences and early reading achievement. *American Journal of Education, 100,* 497-536.

Goodman, Y. (1984). The development of initial literacy. In H. Goelman, A. Oberg & F. Smith (Eds.), *Awakening to literacy.* Exeter, NH: Heinemann.

Goodman, Y. (1986). Children coming to know literacy. In W. Teale & E. Sulzby (Eds.), *Emergent literacy: Writing and reading,* 1-140. Norwood, NJ: Ablex.

Harste, J., Woodward, V. & Burke, C. (1984). *Language stories and literacy lessons.* Portsmouth, NH: Heinemann.

Leichter, H. (1974). Some perspectives on the family as educator. *Teachers College Record, 76,* 198-225.

National Assessment of Educational Progress. (1981). *Reading, thinking, writing: A report on the 1979-1980 assessment.* Denver, CO: NAEP.

National Assessment of Educational Progress. (1985). *The reading report card: Progress toward excellence in our schools.* Princeton, NJ: Educational Testing Service.

Purcell-Gates, V. (1988). Lexical and syntactic knowledge of written narrative held by well-read-to kindergarteners and second graders. *Research in the Teaching of English, 22,* 128-60.

Purcell-Gates, V. (1995). *Other people's words.* Cambridge, MA: Harvard University Press.

Scollon, R. & Scollon, S. (1981). *Narrative, literacy, and face in interethnic communication.* Norwood, NJ: Ablex.

Shimron, J. (1994). The making of readers: The work of Professor Dina Feitelson. In D. Dickinson (Ed.), *Bridges to literacy: Children, families, and schools,* 80-102. Cambridge, MA: Blackwell.

Snow, C. (1993). Families as social context for literacy development. In C. Daiute (Ed.), *The development of literacy through social interaction,* 11-24. San Francisco: Jossey-Bass.

Snow, C., Barnes, W., Chandler, J., Goodman, I. & Hemphill, L. (1991). *Unfulfilled expectations: Home and school influences on literacy.* Cambridge, MA: Harvard University Press.

Snow, C. & Kurland, B. (in press). Sticking to the point: Talk about magnets as a preparation for literacy. In D. Hicks (Ed.), *Child discourse and social learning: An interdisciplinary perspective.* New York: Cambridge University Press.

Svensson, A.K. (1994). Helping parents help their children: Early language stimulation in the child's home. In D. Lancy (Ed.), *Children's emergent literacy: From research and practice,* 79-92. Westport, CT: Praeger.

Taylor, D. & Dorsey-Gaines, C. (1988). *Growing up literate: Learning from inner-city families.* Portsmouth, NH: Heinemann.

Toomey, D. & Sloane, J. (1994). Fostering children's literacy development through parent involvement: A five-year program. In D. Dickinson (Ed.), *Bridges to literacy: Children, families, and schools,* 129-49. Cambridge, MA: Blackwell.

Whitehurst, G., Galco, F., Lonigan, C., Fischel, J., et al. (1988). Accelerating language development through picture book reading. *Developmental Psychology, 24*(4), 552-59.

Endnote

Some of the material in this paper has appeared previously in Snow et al., 1991, *Unfulfilled expectations*, Chapter 1, and Snow, 1993, "Families as social context for literacy development," in C. Daiute (Ed.), *The development of literacy through social interaction*, pp. 11-24.

Informing Approaches to Serving Families in Family Literacy Programs: Lessons From Other Family Intervention Programs

Robert St. Pierre and Jean Layzer
Abt Associates, Inc.

The task of this paper is to explore how lessons from the research on family intervention programs can be used to improve family literacy programs. Research in the following areas is discussed:

- childhood education;

- adult education and training;

- parenting education; and

- support services.

The paper then offers suggestions for improving family literacy programs.

> *There is substanial evidence that effects on children, and effects on parents are best achieved by services aimed directly at parents. There is only limited evidence that we can achieve effects on children through earlier effects on parents.*

Early Childhood Education

Countless studies of early childhood programs have been conducted over the past three decades. Recent meta-analytic reviews by Barnett (1995) and by Wasik and Karweit (1994), as well as earlier meta-analyses by McKey, et al. (1985), conclude that high-quality, intensive, center-based early childhood programs can make an important difference in the lives of young children. More specifically:

- Preschool programs produce gains of between 4 and 11 IQ points but these gains decline over time; effects on achievement are more persistent (Barnett, 1995);

- Preschool programs produce large effects on grade retention and special education placement (Barnett, 1995); and

- Early intervention programs help children get off to a good start; programs with continued follow-up have long-term benefits for children; and highly intensive interventions (such as the Infant Health and Development Program (IHDP, 1990)) are more effective than less intensive ones (Wasik & Karweit, 1994).

There is little evidence from these reviews that preschool programs have large, direct effects upon parents or that early parent effects mediate later effects on children. This makes sense since few early childhood education programs provide intensive services for parents. Further, Karweit's review (1994) concluded that while preschool programs help, preschool programs alone are not enough to ameliorate the effects of poverty.

Adult Education and Job Training

There are two distinct and relevant literatures in this area: (1) adult education/literacy programs such as federally funded adult basic education, adult secondary education, and English as a second language programs, and (2) job training and welfare-to-work programs.

Adult Education Programs

Most reviews of adult basic education (ABE) programs have concluded that education and training programs have not been able to greatly increase adults' literacy skills or job opportunities (Datta, 1992; Duffy, 1992; Mikulecky, 1992). Adult basic and secondary education programs have high dropout rates and low levels of intensity, making it difficult to see how they can be expected to lead to positive effects (Moore & Stavrianos, 1994). Even when these programs do have significant effects on attainment of a General Educational Development (GED) diploma, the literature seems to indicate that having a GED credential does not relate positively to enhanced skill levels, and is not the economic equivalent of a high school diploma (Murnane & Willett, 1993; Cameron & Heckman, 1993). Recent national studies provide some evidence about potentially effective adult education practices:

- Adults are more likely to be motivated and to achieve more when the curriculum content is well suited to their interests and needs (Webb, et al., 1993).

- Adults in ABE programs with highly individualized curricula do better than those enrolled in programs that are less individualized and more structured (Young, et al., 1994).

- Given the limited amount of time adults spend in class and the limited amount of homework done, "massed practice" (i.e., devote more concentrated time to fewer skill areas) may be most effective.

- Adult literacy programs lag far behind in using newer technologies for instruction, even though several major reports, including a recent Office of Technology Assessment report (OTA, 1993) and a National Center on Adult Literacy technology survey (Harvey-Morgan, et al., 1995), have highlighted the need for such assistance.

- Important predictors of program persistence are the presence and use of client support services (e.g., transportation), placement in day rather than evening classes, programs with high levels of service integration, and membership in teacher-based classrooms rather than largely independent study, and class size of 10 or greater (Young, et al., 1994).

Job Training and Welfare-to-Work Programs

For the past 30 years the federal government has targeted assistance to the welfare population so that they can find work and end their dependency on welfare. Fischer and Cordray (1995) cite as examples President Bill Clinton's 1994 Work and Responsibility Act, the JOBS program of the Family Support Act of 1988, OBRA and TEFRA in 1981 and 1982, Jimmy Carter's Program for Better Jobs and Income in 1977, Richard Nixon's Family Assistance Plan in 1969, the Work Experience and Training Projects in 1964, and the Community Work and Training Program in 1962. Three basic approaches have been used and studied through these and other efforts: (1) the "basic education" approach in which the focus is on provision of education and training, with the hope of building sufficient skills in order that the participant can qualify for and find employment; (2) the "job search" approach which focuses primarily on finding employment; and (3) vocational training and on-the-job training (Gueron & Pauly, 1991).

The most recent and most comprehensive analysis of the effects of job training and welfare-to-work programs (Fischer & Cordray, 1995) reviewed the findings from 65 major evaluations and concluded that job training and search programs have small but real effects on employment, AFDC receipt, and income. The impacts are about a 3 to 5 percentage point difference in employment rate (33 percent in the treatment group vs. 30 percent in the control group) and in AFDC rate (73 percent vs. 71 percent), about a 13 percent-19 percent increase in earnings ($50-$135 per quarter) and a 3 percent to 9 percent decrease in AFDC grants ($50 to $100 per quarter). In addition to these overall findings, the reviewers concluded that:

- Job search interventions had early positive impacts on employment and AFDC while basic education programs had early negative effects followed by later positive effects. Vocational training and on-the-job-training programs had negative effects.

- Impacts are larger for worse-off clients (in terms of education and income), and it is important to match client needs to appropriate services (i.e., basic education, job search, or vocational training).

- Effective program elements include: (1) extensive job development efforts and an emphasis on employment, (2) equal use of job search and basic education approaches, (3) an emphasis on participation and a willingness to use sanctions to enforce participation, and (4) availability of child care.

Perhaps significant for those interested in improving family literacy programs, the reviewers noted that the findings on small effects are not surprising, especially since job training and welfare-to-work interventions address only a few of the many problems faced by the welfare population.

Parenting Education

Parenting education is an integral component of most family intervention programs. The underlying assumptions are that increased knowledge will result in positive changes in parental attitudes toward and behavior with children, and that those changes, in turn, will improve outcomes for children. Of course, these are largely untested assumptions. While there is some evidence that parenting education can produce positive changes in parental attitudes and behavior, there is little evidence of the hoped-for link between changes in parents' attitudes and the actual development of their children. In addition, our understanding of what kinds of parent education are most effective is clouded by the

variety of approaches and the confounding effects of differences in target populations, treatment intensity, and the background and training of providers as well as the additive effects of other program components that may accompany parenting education.

Several rigorously designed studies have found short-term positive effects of parenting education on maternal knowledge, attitudes, and behavior (Johnson & Walker, 1991; Travers, et al., 1982; Andrews et al., 1982; St. Pierre, et al., 1995; Quint, et al., 1994), although there is evidence from some other studies that parenting education is less effective with teen mothers (Pfannenstiel & Seltzer, 1989). A review of 13 randomized trials of home visiting programs for low-income families with infants, which included parenting education as a major component, found mixed impacts on parental attitudes and behaviors (Olds & Kitzman, 1993). Although six of the studies showed small positive program effects on children's cognitive or social-emotional development, in only two of them was this change associated with parental change. The authors also looked at home visiting interventions for families at risk for child abuse or neglect and found no impact on parental behavior overall; however, in two of the six interventions there were positive changes in the caregiving behavior of unmarried teen mothers.

Two experimental studies compared the effectiveness of home-based and center-based parent education (Wasik, et al., 1990; Field, et al., 1982). Both revealed the effects on parent behavior and child development for center-based models only. Since the center-based programs included an early childhood education component, which the parents observed, it is likely that the effects reported are attributable to this component, rather than to the parent education component alone. Barnett (1995) used data from 33 early childhood intervention programs to demonstrate that persistent effects on children's school performance are not attributable to program effects on parents, but rather to early, direct effects on children, themselves.

These studies suggest that while it is possible to use parenting education to increase maternal knowledge, to change attitudes, and possibly to change their behavior with children, parenting education will not, by itself, result in improved child outcomes. This may be because the effects are not large enough or because change in parents occurs too slowly to affect early child outcomes. In addition, there is only limited research support for using paraprofessionals to deliver parent education through home visits, an increasingly popular intervention, if the ultimate outcome is improved child outcomes. It may be that professionals are more likely to interact directly with the children in the course of the home visit, in addition to working with the mother, providing a role model for interaction as well as direct experience for the child. David Olds is currently conducting an experimental test of the relative effectiveness of professional and paraprofessional home visitors.

Support Services

Support services (e.g., transportation, meals, child care, counseling, and many others) play a role in many types of family intervention programs. The rationale is that while such supports may or may not have a direct effect on families, they can remove barriers to participation in the *core* programmatic services. To our knowledge there has been no research specifically on the effectiveness of support services in enhancing participation in more formal program services. Still, anecdotal evidence suggests their importance in different arenas:

- *Adult education*: A recent national evaluation found a strong relationship between client use of support services and hours of instruction received by those clients (Young, et al., 1994).

- *Job training and welfare reform*: A recent meta-analysis cited *barriers to work*, such as lack of transportation and child care, as a reason for the generally small effects of welfare-to-work programs (Fischer & Cordray, 1995).

- *Family literacy*: The national Even Start evaluation concluded that over 80 percent of Even Start projects provided a range of

support services that helped adults and children engage in core service activities (St. Pierre, et al., 1995).

Improving Family Literacy Programs

Based on the evidence presented above, we offer some recommendations for improving family literacy programs.

Aim to Achieve Large Effects

There is no evidence that small, short-term effects on children or adults lead to large, long-term improvements in life chances. On the other hand, some programs which produce large effects on children's preschool performance also have produced large effects later in life. Family literacy programs ought to aim to achieve large effects both with children and adults. This stance implies that it is not worth spending money on family literacy programs unless we have reasonable expectations that they will have large effects.

High-Quality, High-Intensity Services Are Important

There is no evidence that low-quality services lead to large effects. Rather, it is the high-quality, high-intensity programs (e.g., the Perry Preschool Program and the Infant Health and Development Program [IHDP]) which have produced large effects. A high intensity program such as the IHDP uses a carefully specified curriculum to provide a full-week, full-year program for children from 1 to 3 years of age. It has short-term cognitive effects on children which are on the order of five to ten times as large as the effects of low-intensity programs. Further, Wasik and Karweit (1994) concluded that the most effective early childhood interventions included intensive child and parent services that involved a center-based program for children and meetings with parents on a weekly or semi-weekly basis for at least a year. Low-intensity parenting components did not add much, if anything, to the effectiveness of a high-intensity child component.

Many family literacy programs rely on existing local service providers for early childhood education or adult education. This approach is efficient because it avoids duplication of services, but it can only be effective if those services are of a sufficient quality and intensity to produce large effects. Well-run, high-quality Head Start programs ought to be sufficient for early childhood education, but it is much more difficult to find high-quality, high-intensity adult education programs. It often may not be possible to create a high-quality, high-intensity family literacy program from locally existing services.

Do Not Rely on Parenting Education to Produce Child Effects

There is substantial evidence that effects on children are best achieved by services aimed directly at children, and effects on parents are best achieved by services aimed directly at parents. There is only limited evidence that we can achieve effects on children through earlier effects on parents. Thus, it is important for a family literacy program to provide early childhood education services directly for the benefit of children, and not to assume that it is just as good to provide parenting services to mothers who will then act as enhanced intervenors in their children's lives. Ramey, et al. (1995) support this point when they note that even programs with a strong parenting component can require years to produce effects. Under this scenario infants lose out, since they develop for some years without the benefit of high-quality parenting.

Individualize Services

Program designs rarely reflect the fact that adults vary in their capacities and in their deficits. Adults enter adult education and parenting programs with different levels of motivation, knowledge, and skills, as well as with disparate learning styles. Why should they be expected tc progress to the same satisfactory point when exposed for the same amount of time to a single curriculum delivered in a uniform fashion? While many families may benefit from home visits, there

is bound to be variation in the needs of those families such that some need occasional visits by a paraprofessional while others need more frequent visits by a highly trained worker with a teaching style and curriculum tailored to their needs. Program staff often make this point, but the design and costs of local programs often do not allow much flexibility. At the same time there are families who have little need of one of the program components. Even among low-income families, there are intuitively sensitive and competent parents. Must they participate in parenting education as a condition of other assistance?

Use New Technologies

Sometimes what is observed in programs is less telling than what is not observed. In particular, there is little use of new technology in programs for parents. For example, videotaping has been used effectively in one or two parent education programs, but is not widely used. A greater use of computers and new educational software would make possible greater individualization in adult education and family literacy programs.

Combine and Co-Locate Related Program Components

There is evidence suggesting that better effects are achieved when programs for parents and programs for children are located at a single site. We need to take seriously the multiple effects of such a strategy; children see their parents engaged in learning activities and acting as positive role models, and parents observe both their children's learning activities and also see caregivers and teachers modelling developmentally-appropriate behavior. At the same time, parents and children each benefit directly from the program components directed at them.

Conclusions

To conclude, intensive early childhood programs can have positive effects on children; adult education and job training programs produce positive effects on GED attainment, but not on literacy skills, and only small effects on income or employment; and although parenting programs can change parenting skills, there is little research evidence to show that these improved parenting skills have any impact on children. It is suggested that family literacy programs pay attention to the following:

- aim to achieve large effects by delivering high-quality intensive services;

- question the advisability of relying on local service providers which may not be able to deliver high quality services; and

- do not rely on parenting education to produce child effects.

These three suggestions, taken together, should be considered and discussed in the process of providing the best program service possible.

References

Andrews, S.R., Blumenthal, J.B., Johnson, D.L., Kahn, A.J., Ferguson, C.,J., Lasater, T.M., Malone, P.E. & Wallace, D.B. (1982). The skills of mothering: A study of parent child development centers. *Monographs of the Society for Research in Child Development.*, 47, 6, Serial No. 198.

Barnett, W.S. (in press). Long-term effects of early childhood care and education on disadvantaged children's cognitive development and school success. In S. Boocock & W.S. Barnett (Eds.), *Early Childhood Care and Education for Disadvantaged Children: Long-Term Effects.* Albany, NY: SUNY Press.

Cameron, S. & J. Heckman (1993). Nonequivalence of high school equivalents. *The Journal of Labor Economics*, Vol. 11: 1-47.

Datta, L.J. (1992). Youth interventions: Literacy. In T.G. Sticht, M.J. Beeler & B.A. McDonald (Eds.), *The Intergenerational Transfer of Cognitive Skills, Volume 1: Programs, Policy, and Research Issues.* Norwood, NJ: Ablex.

Duffy, T.M. (1992). What makes a difference in instruction? In T.G. Sticht, M.J. Beeler & B.A. McDonald (Eds.), *The Intergenerational Transfer of Cognitive Skills, Volume 1:*

Programs, Policy, and Research Issues. Norwood, NJ: Ablex.

Field, T.M., Widmayer, S.M., Stringer, S. & Ignatoff, E. (1982). Teenage, lower-class, black mothers and their preterm infants: An intervention and developmental follow-up. *Child Development, 51*, 426-36.

Fischer, R.L. & Cordray, D.S. (1995). *Job training and welfare reform: A policy-driven synthesis.* New York: Russell Sage Foundation.

Gueron, J. M. & Pauly, E. (1991). *From welfare to work.* New York: Russell Sage Foundation.

Harvey-Morgan, J., Hopey, C. & Rethmeyer, R. (1995). *Computers, technology, and adult literacy: Results of a national survey on computer technology use in adult literacy programs.* Philadelphia, PA: University of Pennsylvania, National Center on Adult Literacy.

Karweit, N.L. (1994). Can preschool alone prevent early learning failure? In R.E. Slavin, N.L. Karweit & B.A. Wasik (Eds.), *Preventing Early School Failure: Research, Policy, and Practice.* Boston, MA: Allyn and Bacon.

Infant Health and Development Program (June 13, 1990). Enhancing the outcomes of low-birthweight, premature infants. *Journal of the American Medical Association*, Vol. 263, no. 22, 3035-3042.

Johnson, D. & Walker, T. (1991). *Final report of an evaluation of the Avance parent education and family support program.* Report submitted to the Carnegie Corporation. San Antonio, TX: Avance.

McKey, R.H., Condelli, L., Granson, H., Barrett, B., McConkey, C. & Plantz, M. (1985). *The impact of Head Start on children, families, and communities.* Washington, DC: CSR, Inc.

Mikulecky, L. (1992). National adult literacy and lifelong learning goals. *National Center on Adult Literacy Newsletter.* Philadelphia: National Center on Adult Literacy.

Moore, M. & Stavrianos, M. (1994). *Adult education reauthorization: Background.* Washington, DC: Mathematica Policy Research.

Murnane, R. & Willett, J. (1993). Do high school dropouts benefit from obtaining a GED? Using multi-level modeling to examine longitudinal evidence from the NLSY.

Unpublished manuscript. Cambridge, MA: Harvard University Graduate School of Education.

Olds, D.L., & Kitzman, H. (1993). Review of research on home visiting for pregnant women and parents of young children. In *The Future of Children: Home Visiting*, Winter, 3, 3:53-92. Center for the Future of Children: The David and Lucile Packard Foundation.

Office of Technology Assessment (1993). *Adult literacy and new technologies: Tools for a lifetime* (OTA-SET-550). Washington, DC: U.S. Government Printing Office.

Pfannenstiel, J. & Seltzer, D. (1989). New parents as teachers: Evaluation of an early parent education program. *Early Childhood Research Quarterly, 4,* 1-18.

Quint, J.C., Polit, D.F., Bos, H. & Cave, G. (1994). *New Chance: Interim findings on a comprehensive program for disadvantaged young mothers and their children.* New York: Manpower Demonstration Research Corporation.

Ramey, C.T., Ramey, S.L., Gaines, K.R. & Blair, C. (1995). Two-generation early intervention programs: A child development perspective. In S. Smith (Ed.), *Two-generation programs for families in poverty: A new intervention strategy.* Norwood, New Jersey: Ablex.

St. Pierre, R., Swartz, J., Gamse, B., Murray, S. & Deck, D. (1995). *National evaluation of the Even Start Family Literacy Program: Final report.* Cambridge, MA: Abt Associates Inc.

Travers, J., Nauta, M. & Irwin, N. (1982). *The effects of a social program: Final report of the Child and Family Resource Program's Infant-Toddler Component.* Cambridge, MA: Abt Associates Inc.

Wasik, B., Ramey, C., Bryant, D. & Sparling, J. (1990) A longitudinal study of two early intervention strategies: Project CARE. *Child Development. 61,* 1682-96.

Wasik, B.A. & Karweit, N.L. (1994). Off to a good start: Effects of birth to three interventions on early school success. In R.E. Slavin, N.L. Karweit, and B.A. Wasik (Eds.) *Preventing Early School Failure: Research, Policy, and Practice.* Boston, MA: Allyn and Bacon.

Webb, L., Sherman, J. & Koloski, J. (1993). A review of research on effective practices in adult education programs. In J. Sherman, *Identifying Effective Adult Education Programs and Practices: Expert Papers and Overview of Reports.* Washington, D.C. Pelavin Associates, Inc.

Young, M., Morgan, M., Fitzgerald, N. & Fleischman, H. (1994). *National Evaluation of Adult Education Programs: Final Report.* Arlington, VA: Development Associates Inc.

Meeting the Needs of Families in Family Literacy Programs

Dorothy Strickland
Rutgers University

Professional educators have long recognized and valued the role of the family in education. However, interest in family literacy as a concept to be studied and analyzed is actually rooted in the work of anthropologists and sociologists who have long studied the family as a general concept (Leichter, 1974). As a discipline, though, family literacy is in its infancy and lacks a widely agreed-upon definition. In its broadest sense, family literacy encompasses both the research and the implementation of programs involving parents, children, and extended family members and the ways in which they support and use literacy in their homes and in their communities.

The lack of a clearly stated definition of family literacy has not diminished interest in exploring it as a means of promoting literacy development in the home, the school, and the workplace. Indeed, increased awareness of the important role of the "family as educator" has sparked a number of federal, state, and local initiatives that provide research on family literacy and family literacy support programs.

This paper focuses on program delivery and collaboration of family literacy programs. It will explore how family literacy programs work and the factors that influence their implementation.

> *Perhaps the best "test" to determine how well program developers link design and development to the perceived needs of participants is by an examination of the adjustments made to programs as those needs are listened to and responded to over a period of time.*

Specifically, it attempts to answer the following questions:

- How are the social and educational needs of families in a community perceived and identified?

- How are the design and development of family literacy programs related to such needs?

Before discussing the questions, themselves, it is necessary to provide a background on some of the assumptions and controversies regarding the topic. This will provide a context and a rationale for determining why these questions are so important.

Family Literacy: Some Widely Held Assumptions

Whether implicitly or explicitly stated, certain perceptions about families and the development of family literacy seem to pervade discussions about programs. Such beliefs have so far played an influential role in the planning and implementation of family literacy programs, as perceptions serve to inform the decisions made about what is "good" or "bad" for families.

More fundamentally, widely held assumptions provide an added impetus for the family literacy movement, itself. It is important to note, also, that, as used *here*, the term *family* is broadly defined to include a range of individuals who live together and function in a more or less traditionally familial way; the term *parent* refers to anyone fulfilling the responsibilities usually associated with the parent of a child or children over a sustained period of time. The following are some of these key assumptions:

• *Most families seek to improve the general conditions of their lives by:*

— seeking economic self-sufficiency and general well-being;

— setting up goals of self-sufficiency and general well-being as desirable for individual families and for the common good of the community; and

— realizing that some families are at greater risk than others of not attaining their goals for improvement.

A related assumption is that society (specifically government) has a role in supporting family goals for a better life.

• *Most families make special efforts to improve the lives of their children, especially in terms of:*

— wanting what is best for their children;

— functioning as the first and most important *educators* of their children;

— understanding and acting upon their role in building a supportive learning environment for their children, thus benefiting the entire family;

— taking advantage of opportunities for self-improvement and learning, again, benefiting the entire family; and

— seeking help in creating a positive learning environment at home.

• *Literacy plays a major role in the achievement of family goals, especially in terms of the following realities:*

— viewing attainment and improvement of literacy positively in our society;

— families' differing in their perceptions of how literacy is attained and improved;

— socio-cultural factors having a strong influence on how families pursue their literacy goals; and

— acknowledging that all families have a culture of learning that is worthy and useful in the attainment of their own literacy goals.

(Partly based on a list generated at the Research Design Symposium on Family Literacy, September 7-8, 1995, Office of Educational Research and Improvement, Washington, D.C.)

Family Literacy: Who Is Doing What for Whom and Why?

Although the assumptions listed above can be applied to *all* families, they take on a sense of urgency when applied to those families considered most in need. Thus, virtually all of the programs within the realm of family literacy have been targeted toward low-income populations in which literacy achievement has consistently lagged behind that of their mainstream counterparts. At the federal level, family literacy programs are tied to The Adult Education Act (Titles II and III), The Library and Construction Act (Titles I and VI), The Head Start Act, The Family Support Act of 1988 (Title IV-A), and several programs in the Elementary and Secondary Education Act, including Chapter 1; Even Start; Title VII Bilingual Education; and Title III, Part B, the Family School Partnership Program. Similarly, at the state and local levels almost all programs are targeted toward those families for whom the need is perceived to be the greatest. The perception of need has been verified by all of the usual determinants, including low income, high unemployment, and chronic school failure. In much of the legislation, guidelines for the use of such funds were established on the basis of these kinds of demographics.

The three issues of greatest concern to the National Center for Family Literacy upon its inception in 1989 continue to be typical of most family literacy programs today:

- low level of literacy skills possessed by a large percentage of our adult population;

- growing number of children living in impoverished, disadvantaged homes and failing in school; and

- rapid increase in the level of literacy required for employment.

It is not surprising that most of those involved in family literacy programs were delighted with the new efforts toward supporting families in this way. However, as time went on, others began to worry about the growing and widespread impression that the concept of family literacy really implied *family illiteracy* and that it was only applicable to low socio-economic and minority groups.

Although commending the excellent accomplishments of many family literacy programs, some stakeholders expressed concern about what they considered to be an emerging "deficit model" of family literacy. This model appeared to be designed primarily to *fix* families or to "make them over" in some predetermined way with seemingly little investigation of the perceived needs of the families involved or regard for the socio-cultural community of which the families were a part. In the report of New Jersey's Council on Adult Education and Literacy (1993), Florio and Strickland acknowledged the need to concentrate limited resources on families in greatest need, but added:

The Council differs with the National Center's view of Family Literacy policy by concluding that the encouragement and promotion of family literacy must go beyond those families who are perceived as at risk. The Council strongly believes that family literacy programs are not required by disadvantaged families alone, but are important for all families (p. 15).

Other criticisms of family literacy programs go well beyond the need for broadening the audience and application, to concerns about the nature of some intervention programs. Family literacy programs that *train* parents how to interact with their children (to elicit certain types of literacy

outcomes) have been criticized as ignoring the naturally occurring literacy events that exist in virtually all households—as well as the opportunities to make use of what families bring to the learning situation as potential building blocks for literacy development (Anderson & Stokes, 1984; Erickson, 1989; and Taylor & Dorsey-Gaines, 1988).

Morrow and Neuman (1995) acknowledge that: ". . . there is evidence that many low-income, minority, and immigrant families cultivate rich contexts for literacy development and that they support family literacy with effort and imagination" (p. 550). Also, Paratore and Harrison (1995) remind us that "literate practices are present in all families, but that these practices are sometimes incongruent with the uses of literacy in schools" (p. 516).

It should be pointed out that at least one researcher (Edwards, 1995) has responded to the criticism of highly structured parent training programs by pointing out that ". . . we only have the researchers' fears, doubts, and reservations." Edwards suggests that parent voices, perceptions, and evaluations of the programs be highlighted, rather than downplayed (p. 562). Interestingly enough, both Edwards and those who speak out against parent-training programs would argue that the voices of parents and their perceptions be made more visible in family literacy programs that purport to stand for what parents need and want.

Not surprisingly, as a new area of research and programmatic effort, family literacy is in the process of redefining itself. This process is both healthy and natural and should not be construed as a refutation of existing practice. Rather, it should be viewed as an opportunity to engage in the thoughtful reflection and examination needed to improve and extend existing efforts and to make the best use of available resources. No doubt this process will continue in the coming years as programs mature and come under scrutiny.

There also is no doubt that the questions related to program delivery and collaboration explored in this paper will be central to any future discourse.

The following section, therefore, outlines descriptions of some of the most widely known family literacy programs. This is followed by a discussion of how the social and educational needs of families in a community are perceived and identified, and how those needs are related to program design and development.

Family Literacy Programs: A Look at the Perception of Needs

The following sources were used to examine the perception of needs in family literacy programs: *Family Literacy in Action* (Nickse, 1989); *The Reading Teacher* (1989); and *The Journal of Reading* (April, 1995). Both of the journals used published theme issues devoted to the topic of family literacy. *The Reading Teacher* is geared to elementary school teachers and reading specialists; *The Journal of Reading* is geared to middle and secondary school educators and those involved in adult literacy programs. Both journals are published by the International Reading Association.

Below, also, are brief descriptions of all of the programs in *Family Literacy in Action*, including information about how the programs were initiated and how needs were identified and addressed. In the interest of space, summaries of only two journal articles are included, both representative of those articles in both journals that actually describe family literacy programs. The profiles provided are based entirely on the information presented in the reviews. In each case, it is assumed that the programs were selected for inclusion in these publications because they were representative, if not exemplary, in nature.

Programs Listed in *Family Literacy in Action*

Marin County Library Family Literacy Program
Brief Description: home based. Involves non-English-speaking adults and their families in a variety of home- and school-based intergenerational activities. *Identification of needs:*

initiated by volunteer tutor, who noticed that many farm workers' children were falling behind children of Anglo background. Parents recruited through basic-English tutors and by teachers in elementary schools. *Implementation:* provides at-home tutoring and bookmobile services. Extends services to evening/amnesty/ citizenship classes; attempts to link home with school services.

Beginning with Books
Brief Description: library based. Includes a variety of early intervention literacy programs aimed at promoting reading as a part of everyday family life. *Identification of needs:* parents participating in adult literacy program were surveyed to determine why they sought help with literacy. Interest in helping their children with literacy and the need for child care during their own literacy improvement sessions were revealed. *Implementation:* the Read Together Program was designed to provide literacy activities for children while their parents receive literacy services. Transportation is provided as well as a range of library services to parent and child.

Parent Readers Program
Brief Description: higher education based. An intergenerational literacy program for parents enrolled in adult basic education (remedial reading) classes on a college campus. *Identification of needs:* instructors' observations regarding student apathy about their own learning, but expressing apparent deep concern for the learning of their children. *Implementation:* workshops are held for students in which they are introduced to children's literature and strategies for sharing with their children.

Motheread, Inc.
Brief Description: primarily prison based. Intergenerational literacy project for incarcerated women. *Identification of needs:* developed in response to "low literate adults wanting to improve their literacy skills in order to read to their children." *Implementation:* parents attend classes in which children's books are introduced along with a comprehension or critical thinking skill activity. Materials are made available during inmates' visits with their children. (The program also has been adapted to sites other than prisons.)

Project Will

Brief Description: university based. An intergenerational program offering one-on-one reading instruction to low-literate women while providing free child care. *Identification of needs:* survey revealed that more than half of the county's illiterate adults were women and that the lack of child care was preventing them from taking advantage of existing literacy services. Goals of participants vary, including GED objectives and beyond. *Implementation:* women participate in small group and one-to-one tutoring sessions while their children are offered a variety of learning experiences. Parent training is geared to student goals.

Kenan Family Literacy Project

Brief Description: community based (may use public school site). Aimed at improving parents' basic skills and attitudes toward education. *Identification of needs:* outreach program recruits parents with low literacy skills and deemed "at risk." *Implementation:* involves four basic components—early childhood education for the children, adult education, parenting education, and a pre-employment/self-esteem/job readiness component. Parents and children participate three days a week.

Mothers' Reading Program

Brief Description: community based (Settlement House). Adult literacy program, largely English as a Second Language (ESL) for mothers of children attending Head Start. *Identification of needs:* mothers learn of the program upon enrollment of their children. *Implementation:* mothers attend classes focusing on ESL, using reading and writing of their original texts as well as children's literature. Some activities involve children.

Take Up Reading Now (TURN)

Brief Description: community based. Provides basic reading and writing instruction and other support activities to adults. Helps parents develop learning strategies for their children and awareness of educational resources. Offers some joint activities with children. *Identification of needs:* need is based on demographic data regarding illiteracy in the area served. *Implementation:* comprised of three distinct programs—a program that assists parents in

becoming advocates for children experiencing difficulties at school; a program for the collection and dissemination of children's books; and a program that shows parents how they can become their child's first teacher.

In these summaries of family literacy programs, little was explicitly stated about the perceived needs of families. However, there was some evidence that needs were, indeed, considered. For instance, the Marin County Library program did report an attempt to adjust to needs as the program progressed. Also, the Beginning with Books program reported some attempt to do a needs survey at the outset of its project. Needs were expressed most often in terms of the project's goals to address existing problems related to illiteracy. Program development closely followed those needs, according to program administrators.

Programs Described in *The Reading Teacher*, April 1995

Of the seven articles focusing on family literacy in this themed issue, two were specifically devoted to the description of family literacy programs. Both programs were school based. The Pulaski Elementary School family literacy program was designed to help develop self-esteem in children at an early age through parental encouragement and support of their literacy development. The program consists of a series of parent workshops involving demonstrations and small group discussions around issues of concern. Activities that involve parents in their child's literacy education at home and involve them in the school program are also integral to the program.

Project FLAME—Family Literacy: Aprendiendo, Mejorando, Educando (Learning, Bettering, Educating) provides literacy training to parents not yet proficient in English so they can support their children's literacy learning. It also includes a parents-as-teachers component in which parents learn to select books and share them with their children and learn how to use the library.

Like the programs described in *Family Literacy in Action*, these school-based efforts initially grew out of needs perceived by the program administrators—in this case, the school. In each instance, the school personnel sought to bring together what is known about home school partnerships and the need to support the literacy development of students obviously in need of such help. Both projects were set in low socio-economic areas where the populations were largely immigrants and minorities. Also, like some of the previous programs described, more was implied about parent input than was actually stated. However, in the case of these two school-based programs, there was some specific evidence that the needs of parents were directly considered. For example, in their report of the Pulaski program, Come and Fredericks (1995) state that, ". . . [t]he key ingredient to the success of the program was the involvement of parents in the planning" (p. 567). In the case of project FLAME, the developers appeared to be extremely sensitive to the cultural and linguistic background of this community of Spanish speakers. Ironically, this sensitivity actually caused them to alter instruction in a way that was counter to their beliefs about good teaching.

"At times, parents' preconceptions are too strong to overcome. We do not support the use of prescriptive grammar study or workbooks in language learning, but to some parents these approaches are synonymous with good teaching. After a few months of working on language in social contexts, they complained that we weren't really teaching English. We agreed to spend some part of each lesson on worksheets. Eventually, parents saw how wasteful and unnecessary this was, but without such responsiveness it is hard to imagine the program being as successful." (Shanahan, Mulhern & Rodriguez-Brown, 1995, p. 589)

In contrasting the programs listed in *Family Literacy in Action*, published in 1990, with those in *The Reading Teacher*, published in 1995, it is important to note that the latter were described in detail while the former were only summarized. The time span between these reports is also significant. No doubt those who initiate programs today are much more conscious of the concerns voiced by those who complain about deficit-model family literacy programs.

Family Literacy Programs: Relating Development to Need

How are the social and educational needs of families and communities perceived and identified? How are the design and development of family literacy programs related to such needs?

It is clear that the primary sources for determining and articulating needs in a family literacy program are the agencies that implement such a program. In each case, some person or persons felt the need to bring together their knowledge and perceptions of the needs of families deemed at risk of literacy failure. These perceptions are grounded in the day-by-day observations of those who have the power and the will to initiate such programs, and they are supported by demographic data regarding socio-economic status, employment, and school achievement. In some cases, the family literacy programs were planned as an adjunct to existing programs. In others, they were initiated as stand-alone programs in order to provide assistance where those who were in a position to do so had observed a need.

This is not to say that parents and other community members were never consulted informally about their perception of need. It merely suggests that the articulation of needs is largely the responsibility of those who write the grants and administer the programs. Systematic surveys of needs are either rare or not reported in the literature. To those who initiate and administer family literacy programs, the needs may appear so overwhelming that an assessment would only confirm the obvious. The questions posed here about the perception of needs, however, may be another matter. While there is little question about whether or not a need exists, there is some question about how the clients themselves view these needs. What is their take on the obvious?

Some would argue that it is unrealistic to expect parents to take the initiative in programs of the types described here. Each requires expertise both in administration and instruction. They also require funding of some type. Since the very populations being addressed are among the most needy socio-economically and educationally, it is unlikely that they would either demand or initiate such programs on their own. As Shanahan et al. (1995) point out, "Latino families, despite low economic status, are highly concerned about the success of their children, though they are often uncertain how to negotiate the American educational system" (p. 587).

Nevertheless, it is reasonable to expect that programs would attempt to tap the perspective of their clients in some way as they plan and implement their programs. This is implied in some descriptions and left out completely in most others. Thus, it is often difficult to determine the degree to which parents helped plan the programs or shaped the direction of the programs once they are in place. The lack of attention to this is perhaps even more significant when programs claim to be partnerships. Indeed, the term "partnership" may be a reality in some cases. However, failure to mention how control is shared would imply that the partnership is either something to which they aspire or not a high priority.

As expressed in the reports of family literacy programs, development appears highly related to needs. This is not surprising, since the articulation of needs is largely the function of program administrators, and programs are often funded by outside agencies that require a close match between goals and implementation. But whether or not they seek outside funding, program developers must state their objectives and how they will be met. Perhaps the best "test" to determine how well program developers link design and development to the perceived needs of participants is by an examination of the adjustments made to programs as those needs are listened to and responded to over a period of time.

Summary and Conclusions

The literature reveals a growing body of information regarding family literacy and a growing number of highly successful family literacy programs. The overwhelming need for such programs and the pressure for funding have resulted in programs that are largely planned and implemented by those who, although close to the point of need, are not necessarily as collaborative with the target population as they might be. Some critics are concerned by the absence of the voice of the target population and the expression of their perceived needs.

Recent literature indicates that there may be a growing trend toward more flexibility and attention to community perceptions of need and greater efforts toward program flexibility in adjusting to those needs. Following are some conclusions and suggestions:

- Family literacy programs must overtly ground their efforts in needs as perceived by the communities they serve.

- Once a potential program is conceived, specific plans should be outlined to engage the target population in the planning process (e.g., interviews, discussion groups, community surveys, and so on).

- Plans also should include both informal and formal systematic opportunities for collaborative review and reflection on the part of all participants.

- Planning should highlight and build on the strengths of the community to be served. Opportunities for participants to contribute their ideas and efforts, in whatever way feasible, would promote a sense of collaboration and ownership.

- With limited resources, programs should be targeted to the most needy. However, attempts to link projects with ongoing efforts in the general population are desirable. Parents need to know that family literacy is something that is a priority for the entire population. Programs should be aware that, although they and their community are unique in many ways, the problems these programs are addressing are universal in nature.

References

Anderson, A.B., & Stokes, S.J. (1984). Social and institutional influences on the development and practice of literacy. In H. Goelman, A. Oberg, & F. Smith (Eds.), *Awakening to Literacy*, 24-37. Exeter, NH: Heinemann.

Come, B. & Fredericks, A.D. (1995). Family literacy in urban schools: Meeting the needs of at-risk children. *The Reading Teacher*, 48, 566-70.

Edwards, P.A. (1995). Empowering low-income mothers and fathers to share books with young children. *The Reading Teacher*, 48, 558-64.

Erickson, F. (1989). Forward: Literacy risks for students, parents, and teachers. In Allen & J. Mason (Eds.), *Risk Makers, Risk Takers, Risk Breakers: Reducing the Risks for Young Literacy Learners*, xiii-xvi. Portsmouth, NH: Heinemann.

Florio, L. & Strickland, D.S. (1993). *Adult literacy in New Jersey: A report of the Council on Adult Education and Literacy.* Trenton, NJ: New Jersey Department of Labor.

Leichter, H. (1974). Families as environments for literacy. In H. Goelman, A. Oberg, & F. Smith (Eds.), *Awakening to Literacy*, 38-50. Portsmouth, NH: Heinemann.

Morrow, L.M. & Neuman, S.B. (1995). Introduction: Family literacy. *The Reading Teacher*, 48, 550-51.

Nickse, R.S. (1990). *Family literacy in action: A survey of successful programs.* Syracuse, NY: New Readers Press.

Paratore, J. & Harrison, C. (1995). A themed issue on family literacy. *Journal of Reading*, 38, 516-17.

Shanahan, T., Mulhern, M. & Rodriguez-Brown (1995). Project FLAME: Lessons learned from a family literacy program for linguistic minority families. *The Reading Teacher*, 48, 586-93.

Taylor, D. & Dorsey-Gaines, C. (1988). *Growing up Literate.* Portsmouth, NH: Heinemann.

Appendix A

List of Symposium Participants

Authors of Commissioned Papers
Judith Alamprese, *COSMOS Corporation*
Richard Durán, *University of California, Santa Barbara*
Vivian L. Gadsden, *National Center on Fathers and Families*
Beth Harry, *University of Miami*
Andrew Hayes, *University of North Carolina, Wilmington*
Jean Layzer, *Abt Associates*
Larry Mikulecky, *Indiana University, Bloomington*
Douglas Powell, *Purdue University*
Dorothy Strickland, *Rutgers University*
Patton Tabors, *Harvard University*

Respondents (Practitioners)
Gus Estrella, *United Cerebral Palsy Associations*
Delia Garcia, *Florida International University*
Charles Geboe, *Bureau of Indian Affairs*
Howard Miller, *Prince George's County, Maryland, Even Start Project*
Fran Tracy-Mumford, *Delaware Adult and Community Education*

PLLI and ECI Staff
Ann Benjamin, *ECI*
David Boesel, *PLLI*
Veda Bright, *ECI*
Naomi Karp, *ECI*
Teresita Kopka, *PLLI*
Jerome Lord, *PLLI*

Pelavin Research Institute Staff
Rita Kirshstein
Rebecca Shulman
Lenore Webb

Other Observers and Participants
Sharon Darling, *National Center for Family Literacy*
David Fleishman, *National Center for Learning Disabilities*
Gail Houle, *Office of Special Education Programs*
Ann Kornblet, *Learning Disabilities Association of America*
Rhea Lawson, *University of Wisconsin*
Columbus (Chris) Lee, *Office of Vocational and Adult Education*
Mary Lovell, *Office of Vocational and Adult Education*
Robert W. Marley, *National Educational Research Policy and Priorities Board*
Marcia Martin, *U.S. Department of Housing and Urban Development*
Patricia McKee, *Grants Administration, U.S. Department of Education*
William Mehojah, *Bureau of Indian Affairs*
Joyce Muhlestein, *National Educational Research Policy and Priorities Board*
Mercedes Pérez de Colón, *Avance-Hasbro National Family Resource Center*
Eve Robins, *National Adult Literacy and Learning Disabilities Center*
Sharon P. Robinson, *Assistant Secretary, Office of Educational Research and Improvement*
Sheila Smith, *Foundation for Child Development*
Lori Connors Tadros, *Johns Hopkins University*
Susan Thompson-Hoffman, *Office of the Under Secretary, U.S. Department of Education*
Barbara Wasik, *University of North Carolina at Chapel Hill*
Bayla F. White, *Office of Migrant Education, U.S. Department of Education*

Appendix B

Biographical Sketches of Commissioned Authors

Judith Alamprese

Judith Alamprese is a director at COSMOS Corporation in Bethesda, Maryland, where she is responsible for initiatives in adult education, policy analysis, and job training. She has led numerous research and evaluation projects in the fields of adult literacy and basic skills program effectiveness, workplace literacy, interagency coordination, and state assessment systems. Her early work in adult education includes the development of the National External Diploma Program, the first competency-based, applied-performance high school diploma for adults. She was also a member of the research team at the Family Development Research Center, one of the early family intervention programs for at-risk families.

The topic of interagency collaboration has been an ongoing focus of Ms. Alamprese's research, which has included studies of community task forces created as part of the Project Literacy U.S. media campaign and of state and local coordination of adult education funding and services. Currently, Ms. Alamprese is assessing the outcomes from the interagency staff development projects funded by the National Institute for Literacy, and is evaluating the operation of education and business partnerships funded by the National Workplace Literacy Program. She also is studying the development of state infrastructures for family literacy in collaboration with the National Center for Family Literacy. Ms. Alamprese's recent publications include reports on the implementation of the National Literacy Issues Forums in adult basic education programs, and the development of client satisfactory progress standards for Connecticut's welfare reform program.

Richard Durán

Richard Durán is Professor of Education in the Graduate School of Education, University of California, Santa Barbara. He received his Ph.D. in Psychology from the University of California at Berkeley in 1977, specializing in the areas of quantitative and cognitive psychology. He worked as a Research Scientist at Educational Testing Service from 1977-1984 prior to joining the U.C.–Santa Barbara faculty.

Dr. Durán conducts research on literary acquisition of language minority children and families. His research in these areas is sponsored by the Center for Research on Education of Students Placed At Risk, the National Center for Research on Cultural Diversity and Second Language Learning, and the National Center for Research on Evaluation, Standards, and Student Testing. He edited a special issue of the journal *Discourse Processes* (January-February 1995) on the topic of literacy among Hispanics. His recent publications include *Verbal Comprehension and Reasoning Skills of Latino Students,* and *Cooperative Learning Interaction and Construction of Activity.*

Vivian L. Gadsden

Vivian L. Gadsden is Co-Director of the National Center on Fathers and Families, and is an Assistant Professor of Education at the University of Pennsylvania. Since 1990 she has served as Associate Director of the National Center on Adult Literacy at the University of Pennsylvania. Dr. Gadsden's research focuses on family development and literacy across the life-span and examines issues of race, gender, culture, and poverty within the context of intergenerational learning. Among her current research projects are a multigenerational study of family development and literacy within 25 African American families (funded by the Spencer Foundation and the National Academy of Education) and a parent-child Head Start project (supported by the National Center on Adult Literacy). Her recent work appears in *Teachers College Record*, *Urban Education,* and *Theory Into Practice.* Co-editor (with Daniel Wagner) of *Literacy Among African American Youth* (Hampton Press), Dr. Gadsden is completing a booklength volume entitled *Passages in Time,* based on her multigenerational study.

Beth Harry

Beth Harry entered the field of special education as a parent of a child with cerebral palsy. She is now Associate Professor of Special Education at the University of Miami, Florida, and her particular interest is in families and cultural issues. Dr. Harry's research and teaching focus on the impact of culture and social status on the needs and perspectives of families of children with disabilities, and on professionals' interactions with such families. Dr. Harry uses ethnographic research methods to investigate these issues, with particular regard to African American and Hispanic parents. She is the author of *Cultural Diversity, Families and the Special Education System,* a study of Puerto Rican parents' perspectives, and of several articles published in leading educational journals.

Andrew Hayes

Andrew Hayes teaches education administration and instructional design and evaluation at the University of North Carolina at Wilmington. He has his doctorate in educational administration from the University of Georgia, and his master's degree from Louisiana Polytechnic University in the same field. At the University of North Carolina, Dr. Hayes coordinated planning for the master's degree programs in educational leadership, and coordinated planning for a proposed doctoral program in educational leadership. Dr. Hayes served as Principal Investigator of the William R. Kenan, Jr. Charitable Trust Family Literacy Project Evaluation for the National Center for Family Literacy. He also assisted the Governor's Office of Children and Youth of Hawaii in adoption of family literacy as a state strategy. Dr. Hayes has published over 50 project reports, monographs, articles, and conference presentations on topics such as institutes for delinquents, assessment and change of school climate, planning and evaluation, research methods, decision-making processes, instructional design, and family literacy. He is a member of the American Educational Research Association, American Evaluation Association, Eastern Educational Research Association, North Carolina Association for School Administrators, and Southern Regional Council on Educational Administration.

Jean Layzer

Jean Layzer is a Senior Associate at Abt Associates Inc. For the past 20 years she has studied programs and policies that promote the welfare of young children and their families. Most recently, she directed a national study of early childhood programs for disadvantaged preschoolers and an evaluation of Project Giant Step, an innovative program for four-year-olds and their families in New York City. She currently directs a national study of family support programs and is involved in studies of Head Start health services, Head Start Family Service Centers, and the Comprehensive Child Development Program.

Larry Mikulecky

Larry Mikulecky is Professor of Education and chair of the Language Education Department at Indiana University at Bloomington. He received his doctorate from the University of Wisconsin and a master's degree from John Carroll University. Mikulecky is a member of Phi Beta Kappa and has been awarded Indiana University's Gorman teaching award as well as its highest teaching award, the Frederic Bachman Lieber Distinguished Teaching award. He is also recipient of Laubach of Canada's Distinguished Service Award and the state of Indiana's Community Service Award for literacy work.

Dr. Mikulecky's research examines the literacy requirements for success in business, the military, universities, and secondary schools. His most recent research has examined assessment issues in adult literacy programs, workplace literacy programs, and family literacy programs. He has served as principal investigator on over 20 research projects funded by the U.S. Departments of Education and Labor as well as foundation and corporate sponsorship. Dr. Mikulecky has published more than 100 journal articles, textbook chapters, and textbooks. He is lead author on the recent Simon & Schuster series *Strategic Skill Builders for Banking* as well as the basic skills series *On the Job*, published by Cambridge Publications. He has also been Project Director for nearly a dozen Computer Assisted Instruction study skills programs designed for college students with funding from the federal government and corporate sponsors. He is currently directing the National Center on Adult Literacy's Workplace Literacy Impact Evaluation studies.

Douglas Powell

Douglas Powell is Professor and Head of the Department of Child Development and Family Studies at Purdue University, West Lafayette, Indiana. His primary areas of research interest are early childhood and parent educational support programs, and families as learning environments. Currently he directs a research and demonstration project focused on parents' use of inquiry and connections with nonfamilial institutions as strategies for facilitating children's learning. He is a former Editor of the *Early Childhood Research Quarterly* and member of National Education Goals Panel technical resource groups for goals focused on school readiness and school-family partnerships. He is past chair of the Early Education and Child Development Special Interest Group of the American Educational Research Association. One of his recent publications is *Enabling Young Children to Succeed in School* (AERA, 1995).

Catherine Snow

Catherine Snow received her Ph.D. in psychology from McGill University in 1971, after which she worked for several years in the linguistics department of the University of Amsterdam. Her early research focused on the features of children's social and linguistic environments that facilitated language development; cross-cultural differences in mother-child interaction; and factors affecting second language acquisition. Since moving to the Harvard Graduate School of Education in 1978, she has done research on the factors affecting the acquisition of literacy (co-authoring *Unfulfilled Expectations: Home and School Influences on Literacy* with W. Barnes, J. Chandler, I. Goodman, and L. Hemphill), and on the relationships between aspects of oral language development and later literary achievement, in the Home School Study of Language and Literacy Development. She has also pursued these topics in work with multilingual children, including 150 second-through fifth-graders at the United Nations International School and both elementary and middle school children in bilingual programs in New Haven, Connecticut.

Dr. Snow has written about language policy issues in the United States and in developing nations, and was co-editor with Courtney Cazden of *English Plus: Issues in Bilingual Planning in Preschool Education*, a report to UNICEF. She serves on the National Research Council Panel to establish a research agenda for Limited English Proficient and Bilingual Children. Currently, she is the Henry Lee Shattuck Professor of Education in the Department of Human Development and Psychology at the Harvard Graduate School of Education.

Robert St. Pierre

Robert St. Pierre is a Vice President at Abt Associates Inc., where for the last 20 years he has been principal investigator for educational research, evaluation, and policy analysis projects spanning diverse areas such as family literacy, family support, child development, compensatory education, curricular interventions, school health education, and child nutrition. He has published widely in evaluation and educational research journals, and is active in the American Evaluation Association. He currently directs national evaluations of the Even Start Family Literacy Program and the Comprehensive Child Development Program.

Dorothy Strickland

Dorothy Strickland is the State of New Jersey Professor of Reading. She was formerly the Arthur I. Gates Professor of Education at Teachers College, Columbia University. She has also served on the faculties of Kean College of New Jersey and Jersey State College. She taught in the New Jersey public schools for 11 years, six as a classroom teacher and five as a reading consultant and learning disabilities specialist.

Dr. Strickland has her M.A. and Ph.D. from New York University. She received her B.S. at Newark State College. She has authored more than 100 publications. Her books include *Language, Literacy and the Child; Emerging Literacy: Young Children Learn to Read and Write; Educating Black Children: America's Challenge;* and *Families: An Anthology of Poetry for Young Children.* She has also held elective office in both the National Council of Teachers of English and the International Reading Association, where she is past President. She serves on numerous state and national advisory boards.

Dr. Strickland is the recipient of a National Council of Teachers of English award for research, the Rewey Bell Inglis award as Outstanding Woman in English Education, and the International Reading Association's Outstanding Teacher Educator of Reading award. She has been presented with an Honorary Doctorate of Humane Letters from Bank Street College.

Patton Tabors

Patton Tabors is a Research Associate in Education at the Harvard Graduate School of Education. Prior to completing her doctoral degree at Harvard in 1987, Dr. Tabors taught fifth and sixth grades in a variety of inner city settings. She is presently the coordinator for the Home-School Study of Language and Literacy Development, a longitudinal study of the social precursors to literary achievement in children from low-income families. Recent responsibilities have also included directing the Book Reading Project, an embedded observational study of the New Chance and JOBS evaluations for the Manpower Development Research Corporation, which involved assessing the book reading behaviors of over 600 welfare-recipient mothers and their young children.

Dr. Tabors' research interests include first- and second-language acquisition, and the connections between language and literacy development, particularly in low-income populations. She has co-authored a variety of presentations and articles concerning findings from the Home-School Study and the Book Reading Project with Catherine Snow, David Dickinson, and graduate students who have completed thesis work on these data. She is presently writing *Nobody, Yesbody: A Handbook for Early Childhood Educators of Children Learning English as a Second Language.*

ISBN 0-16-048460-X